Twayne's English Authors Series

Sylvia E. Bowman, *Editor*

INDIANA UNIVERSITY

V. Sackville-West

V. Sackville-West

By SARA RUTH WATSON

The Cleveland State University

Twayne Publishers, Inc.   ::   New York

Printed in U.S.A. by
NOBLE OFFSET PRINTERS, INC.
New York, N.Y. 10003

FOR JOHN A. WEIGEL

Preface

Victoria Sackville-West is a novelist in the best English tradition; she is a part of a long heritage that embraces Jane Austen, the Brontës, George Eliot, Virginia Woolf, and Ivy Compton-Burnett. However, her works, once popular in America as well as in Britain, seem largely neglected now. Today, much of her writing seems old-fashioned and quaint. But my intention in this book, the first full-length study of V. Sackville-West, is to establish her position in the mainstream of English literature, particularly in the history of the novel. Moreover, her connections with the Bloomsbury Group, especially with Virginia Woolf, lend a particular interest to her work and to her biography. However, this book is not a biography: it is an attempt to write an introduction to this author and her works with this thesis in mind: to show that she does have a place in the English literary tradition.

Other aims are (1) to list and describe her writings, (2) to present a critical analysis of them, and (3) to evaluate her achievements. The serious student of English literature of the first half of the twentieth century should find this study of value because V. Sackville-West in many ways penetrates to the core of her time-period and presents ideas significant during this era. Even more importantly, she often concerns herself with basic concepts still relevant in our society.

Several problems confronted me in the course of writing this book. Obviously, it is necessary for a scholar to know his subject as well as possible, to identify with the person he is trying to portray; but Miss Sackville-West is not an easy person to understand. Few, if any, came close to her. Even members of her family felt that they did not know her completely. That she was an eccentric is not surprising, for writing is a solitary task. V. Sackville-West herself did not fully reject the label "eccentric," saying that, if to prefer the solitude of Sissinghurst to the society of the world was being eccentric, then she supposed she was.

Another problem that arose was caused by her versatility. She wrote not only poetry and novels but biography, travel-books, scholarly articles, popular pieces on gardening, sports, and so on. As can be seen, there is hardly a genre she did not handle. Obviously, in such an introductory study as this, I could not mention all of her writings. But this author's versatility, in large part, dictated the organization of this study. The opening chapter presents the available biographical material; and, if this section seems long, it is because, for V. Sackville-West, the consciousness of a long, continuing family tradition became an essential quality of her writing and because she used so many of her own experiences in her works. Chapter two discusses her friendship with Virginia Woolf and the influence of the Bloomsbury Group upon V. Sackville-West's ideas and style. I then analyze her work by genre: her non-fiction, her poetry, her short stories, her novels. The final chapter is a summation and an appraisal.

I wish to thank my sister, Miss Emily Watson, for her ready ear, honest criticism, and industrious typing. Without her, this study would never have been written.

SARA RUTH WATSON

The Cleveland State University

Acknowledgments

Curtis Brown, Ltd., for permission to quote from *The Devil At Westease, Joan of Arc, Thirty Clocks Strike the Hour and Other Stories, The Dark Island, Collected Poems, All Passion Spent, The Edwardians, Family History, Pepita.*

Doubleday and Company, Inc., for permission to quote from *Heritage, Grand Canyon, The Eagle and the Dove, Grey Wethers, Daughter of France, Challenge, The Easter Party, The Garden, No Signposts in the Sea, Knole and the Sack-villes, The Heir, Seducers in Ecuador.*

Harcourt Brace and World, Inc., for permission to quote from Virginia Woolf's *Orlando* and *A Writer's Diary.*

Mr. Nigel Nicolson, for permission to quote from *The Land* and the *Diaries and Letters of Sir Harold Nicolson.*

Contents

Chronology

(Dates for books cited are those of the English first edition.)

1892   Victoria Mary Sackville-West born at Knole, March 9; daughter of Lord (third Baron) Sackville and Lady Sackville.

1909   Drama, based on the life of Thomas Chatterton, privately printed.

1913   Married the Honourable Harold Nicolson.

1914   Her first child, Benedict, born.

1915   *Constantinople: Eight Poems.*

1917   *Poems of West and East* (her first genuine publication); son Nigel born.

1919   *Heritage,* her first novel.

1921   "Orchard and Vineyard" (in *Collected Poems*); *The Dragon in Shallow Waters.*

1922   *The Heir: A Love Story; Knole and the Sackvilles.*

1923   *Challenge; Diary of the Lady Anne Clifford* with introduction and notes by V. Sackville-West; *Grey Wethers.*

1924   *Seducers in Ecuador.*

1926   *Passenger to Teheran; The Land.*

1927   *Aphra Behn, the Incomparable Astrea; The Land* awarded the Hawthornden prize.

1928   *Twelve Days: An Account of the Journey across the Bakhtari Mountains in Southwestern Persia.*

1929   *Andrew Marvell;* "The King's Daughter" (in *Collected Poems*); "Women Poets of the 'Seventies" in *Royal Society of Literature of the United Kingdom, XII.*

1930   The Nicolsons move to Sissinghurst. *The Edwardians;* "The Future of the Novel," in *The Week-End Review;* "Aphra Behn," in *Six Brilliant English Women.*

1931   *All Passion Spent; Duineser Elegien.* Poems of Rainer Maria Rilke translated by V. Sackville-West and Edward Sackville-West; "Invitation to Cast Out Care," in *Collected Poems; Sissinghurst.*

1932   *Family History; Thirty Clocks Strike the Hour and Other Stories; The Death of Noble Godavary and Gottfried Künstler.*

1933   *Collected Poems,* Vol. II; lecture tour of the United States with the Honorable Harold Nicolson.

1934   *The Dark Island.*

1935 "Beginnings," in *On Writing Techniques: An Anthology*; *How Does Your Garden Grow?*

1936 *Saint Joan of Arc*; Lady Sackville died, leaving V. Sackville-West a small fortune.

1937 *Pepita*; *Some Flowers*.

1938 *Solitude: A Poem.*

1939 "Walter de la Mare and The Traveler," in *Proceedings of the British Academy*; *Country Notes*.

1940 *Country Notes in Wartime* (first published in *The New Statesmen and Nation*).

1941 "Virginia Woolf," in *Horizon*; *Selected Poems*; *English Country Houses*.

1942 *Grand Canyon.*

1943 *The Eagle and the Dove*; *The Comet: A Poem.*

1944 *The Woman's Land Army* (an account written for the ministry of agriculture); *Les Français Parlent Aux Français: A Poem*; *The Stone Manger: A Poem*; *Searchlights: A Poem.*

1945 *Another World than This*, poetry anthology compiled by V. Sackville-West and the Honourable Harold Nicolson.

1946 *The Garden.*

1947 *The Devil at Westease*; "Outdoor Life," in *The Character of England*; introduction to Alice C. Meynell's *Prose and Poetry*; *Nursery Rhymes.*

1948 Made Companion of Honor; *The Garden* received the Heinemann Prize.

1951 *In Your Garden* (articles from *The Observer*).

1953 *The Easter Party*; *In Your Garden Again.*

1955 "Virginia Woolf and *Orlando*," in *The Listener*; *More for Your Garden*. Received the Veitch Gold Medal of the Royal Horticultural Society.

1958 *Even More for Your Garden*; *A Joy of Gardening.*

1959 *Daughter of France: The Life of Anne Marie Louise D'Orleans (1627-1693).*

1961 *No Signposts in the Sea*; *Faces: Profiles of Dogs.*

1962 Victoria Mary Sackville-West died. Ashes placed in the crypt of Withyham Church.

CHAPTER 1

The Emergence of V. Sackville-West

"She is a dark river moving deeply in shadows."
—Sir Harold Nicolson.[1]

I Antecedents

VICTORIA Sackville-West descended from an ancient and noble house, for the Sackvilles trace their lineage to ninth-century Normandy. About 890, Rollo the Dane and his adventurous Vikings settled about five miles south of Dieppe in a small village which they no doubt aptly named Salcaville, or Sauqueville, because these Northmen "sacked" every town they occupied; and the early governors of this town took the name of Sackville. Although this account of the origin of the name may be purely fictional, the Sackvilles certainly trace their heritage as far back as the Norman Conquest, when a Herbrand de Sackville accompanied William the Conqueror to England. Like most of the Norman feudal lords, he received strong and powerful possessions in the new land and became wealthy.

After Herbrand, the names of many Sackvilles may be found on the pages of English history. But, in addition to their political and social influence, some of these descendants were important in literary history. The first name to catch the attention of the literary historian is that of Sir Richard Sackville, who was influential at the court of Henry VIII and who instigated the writing of *The Scholemaster* by Roger Ascham. This famous early treatise on education developed from a dinner conversation held at Queen Elizabeth's court at Windsor on December 10, 1563; in his preface Ascham calls Sir Richard "That worthy gentleman . . . a lover of learning and all learned men."[2]

The next Sackville to win a place in literary annals is Sir
Richard's son, Sir Thomas Sackville (1536-1608). One of the
"transition" poets, he gained immortality for writing the finest
pieces in *The Mirror for Magistrates* (1563): the "Induction
and Complaint of the Duke of Buckingham." These poems, which
contain some of the earliest nature descriptions in English
poetry, demonstrate that this young Sackville had an eye for
beauty in the English countryside and, in these respects, V.
Sackville-West resembled her illustrious Elizabethan ancestor.
These poems deserve a permanent place in the language. Then,
while a law student at the Inns of Court, he wrote, in collabora-
tion with Thomas Norton, the first English tragedy, *Gorboduc*
(1561). This drama is remarkable in two ways: it introduced
blank verse as the vehicle for tragedy, and its plot was taken
from English history (or pseudo-history). Queen Elizabeth
bestowed upon Sir Thomas the manor-house of Knole, near
Sevenoaks in Kent, which is now a National Trust Estate. Knole
was V. Sackville-West's girlhood home.

The best that can be said of Sir Thomas's grandson, Sir
Richard Sackville, third Earl of Dorset, was that he was a
friend and patron of poets—among them Francis Beaumont,
Ben Jonson, John Fletcher, and Michael Drayton. As for Richard,
fifth Earl of Dorset, V. Sackville-West wrote that he is of no
particular interest except "that he translated *Le Cid* into English
verse and wrote a poem on Ben Jonson."[3] Charles Sackville, the
sixth Earl, became famous or notorious—as a "jolly, loose-living,
magnificent Maecenas. . . . The patron of men of genius and
the dupe of women." He peopled Knole with poets and cour-
tesans; he left for his descendants a room rich with memories
of John Dryden, Alexander Pope, Matthew Prior, and Thomas
Shadwell. Sir Charles wrote "Cavalier" poetry, gay little pastoral
songs, and a rousing ballad composed on the eve of a naval
engagement during the Dutch War of 1665.[4] Many are the
tales told of his escapades by Samuel Pepys and Samuel John-
son, who condemn his antics. Finally, Sir Charles had an affair
with Nell Gwynn.

His son Lionel Sackville, seventh Earl and first Duke of
Dorset, was a much paler figure, and continued only half-
heartedly his father's patronage of the poets. Victoria Sackville-
West gives him short shrift: "Unlike his predecessors or their

descendants, he was neither an ambassador, a poet, nor a patron of art or letters—'I have not,' he wrote, 'genius sufficient for works of mere imagination.' First he was a soldier and then a statesman, both disastrously."[5] Lionel's son, Charles Sackville, second Duke of Dorset, was mad about opera and *prima donnas*. He also dabbled in poetry, all of it bad. And the next Duke of Dorset, John Frederick Sackville, divided his interests between cricket and verse—or, rather, he united them; for his ballad in sixty-five verses celebrates a cricket match between Kent and Surrey.

In the nineteenth century, George John Frederick Sackville, fourth Duke of Dorset, inherited the title when he was only five; however, he died at twenty-one in 1815. His only distinction seems to have been his friendship with Lord Byron, whose "fag" he was at Harrow and who immortalized him in *Hours of Idleness*. After the death of this Sackville, the title of Duke of Dorset went to a distant cousin; but George John's mother, the Duchess, lived at Knole until her death in 1825, at which time her estate devolved upon her two daughters, Mary and Elizabeth. Elizabeth, Victoria's great-grandmother, married John West, Lord de le Warr. When she died in 1870, she willed Buckhurst (the old sixteenth-century home of the Sackvilles) to her elder son and Knole to her younger sons, one of whom, Lionel, was Victoria's grandfather. He never married but remained devoted to his mistress Pepita, the Spanish dancer, the subject of V. Sackville-West's well-known biography.

When Lionel died in 1908, the title and estate went to his nephew Lionel, who became the third Lord Sackville. On June 17, 1890, he married his first cousin, Victoria Josefa Dolores Cataline, the oldest of Pepita's daughters. The marriage was a strange one: Pepita's daughter had much of the Latin temperament, of the volatility, of her mother; and she already had had a strange, adventurous life. Reared in a convent in Paris, she was sent at eighteen to the United States to be her father's official hostess at the British Embassy, an experience which served her well when she became mistress of Knole. Lionel Sackville-West was a Victorian English gentleman—reserved, quiet, antisocial, and, above all, gentle. This ill-mated pair, much in love, became the parents of V. Sackville-West, English novelist.

II *Childhood*

Victoria was born at Knole, March 9, 1892, daughter of the
third Lord and Lady Sackville. At an early age, Victoria sensed
the importance of Knole; for her it was a living symbol of the
continuity of history, of the heritage of a long family-line, of
the everyday life-patterns of past ages—as we see from her
own account of the gardens:

The bowling-green still rises, square and formal, backed by the two
great tulip trees and the more distant woods of the park. The long
perspective of the herbaceous borders was left undisturbed. The
apple-trees in the little square orchards, that bear their blossom and
their fruit from year to year with such countrified simplicity in the
heart of all that magnificence, were not uprooted.... The white
rose which was planted under James I's room has climbed until it
now reaches beyond his windows on the first floor; the great lime
has dropped its branches until they have layered themselves in the
ground of their own accord and grown up again with fresh roots
into three complete circles all sprung from the parent tree, a cloister
of limes, which in summer murmurs like one enormous beehive; the
magnolia outside the Poet's Parlour has grown nearly to the roof,
and bears its mass of flame-shaped blossoms like a giant candelabrum;
the beech hedge is twenty-feet high; four centuries have winnowed
the faultless turf. In spring the wisteria drips its fountains over the
top of the wall into the park. The soil is rich and deep and old. The
garden has been a garden for four hundred years.[6]

This passage reveals her deep feeling for the land, a feeling
that lay at the roots of her being and found expression in almost
all forms of her art. Here, too, is a good example of the artist's
use of professional knowledge in some special area—in V.
Sackville-West's writing it often is gardening. The details selected
are accurate and realistic; the effectiveness of the description
derives much from this specific quality. And her choice of such
words as "candelabrum," "winnowed," and "fountains" adds to
the richness.

At Knole, V. Sackville-West lived mostly with her grandfather, "a queer and silent old man."[7] He disliked visitors and
was generally rude, but grandfather and granddaughter got along
famously. Although he had nothing to say to his guests, he
communicated to a child. Once he told Victoria that there were
underground caves in that part of the estate called "the Wilder-

ness," and, of course, Vita (as her family always called her) went digging among the laurels to try to find an entrance. It is significant that, when her grandfather gave her a tree, she mounted a wooden cannon on it to keep away intruders; perhaps she had inherited some of her grandfather's taciturnity. When she was away, her grandfather wrote her letters in colored chalk; and, when she was home, he always gathered up a plate-full of fruit from the dinner-table, put her name on the plate, and hid it in a drawer of his writing desk. This, Victoria tells us, he never failed to do—even when there were thirty people to dinner in the Great Hall. Here is her own picture of this rela-tionship between these two—the little girl and the old man with the romantic past:

When we were at Knole together I used to go down to his sitting-room in the evening to play draughts with him—and never knew whether I played to please him, or he played to please me—and sometimes, very rarely, he told me stories of when he was a small boy ... I clasped my knees and stared at him when he told me these stories of an age which already seemed so remote, and his pale blue eyes gazed away into the past, and suddenly his shyness would return to him and the clock in the corner would begin to wheeze in preparation to striking the hour, and he would say that it was time for me to go to bed. But although our understanding of one another was, I am sure, so excellent, our rare conversations remained always on similar fantastic subjects, nor ever approached the intimate or the personal.[0]

We deduce that this family attachment meant more to Victoria than did any other. In 1908, when Victoria was sixteen, her grandfather was suffering his last illness; and the family decided that she was to go to Scotland for the summer with an old, family friend and devotee of her mother's, Sir John Murray Scott, a bachelor and art connoisseur, and his sisters. Victoria, unaware that she was being got rid of for the time, was taken on the eve of her departure into her grandfather's little sitting-room "to say goodbye." As she sat there alone with him, she was aware that he gazed at her in a rather strange and particular way: "He, at any rate, knew that he would never see me again; for my own part, I wondered why he left his hand lying so long, so heavily, and so affectionately on my shoulder."[9]

Victoria later remembered one particular day of that summer

in Scotland. She had received a letter, written in a foreign-looking handwriting, and addressed to "The Hon. Vita Sackville-West." Carried away by her admiration for *The Scarlet Pimpernel*, she had written a fan-letter to Baroness Orczy, who had answered. As Vita looked at the salutation, she was embarrassed because she had no right to the title. At that moment one of the sisters of Seery (the family nickname for Sir John Scott) entered to tell Vita of her grandfather's death. When Vita went downstairs to Seery, she found him sobbing uncontrolledly:

I stood looking at that huge Jaeger, sob-shaken bulk, and envied him his power of feeling things so immediately and so acutely. For myself, I couldn't feel anything at all; I was just worried because I had no mourning to put on, because I felt dimly that I ought to telegraph to my mother and didn't know what one said on such occasions, and because I had already begun to wonder whether it would be disrespectful to go fishing that day, or whether I ought to stay at home and perhaps play croquet by myself? It was only when I went upstairs again to my own room and found Baroness Orczy's envelope lying on the dressing table that I realized she had been right in her superscription after all; right, though a little previous. My father was now Lord Sackville—or wasn't he?[10]

From childhood, Victoria had two absorbing passions: a fierce love of Knole and a deep regret at not being a boy. If she had been born a boy, she could have inherited Knole; she could have been freed from the shackles of Edwardian society; and she would have had the opportunity to attend schools and a university and to have studied Greek and Latin literature. Her own recollections of her childhood reveal to us the qualities of masculinity, of an introverted nature, and of a strong, even outraged, sense of individualism and nonconformity. She says in her autobiography that she prided herself on being hardy—as much like a boy as possible. She tells us that she was cruel to other children until she lost nearly all her friends; none of the local boys and girls would come to tea, except those who were her allies and lieutenants. She created an "army," but she was in tears of rage because her khaki suit was not made with trousers. In her own words, she paints a vivid picture of the child Victoria: "I see myself in the garden, feel the familiar cut of my pocket-knife into the wooden table of the summer-house where I did my lessons; see the little cart into which I used to harness three ill-assorted dogs; see myself plain, lean, dark, unsociable, unattractive—horribly unattractive!—rough and secret."[11]

After her grandfather's death, the whole question of the succession of the title and Knole arose; and lawsuits followed. The case was aired in all the papers; Knole was shut up—and each member of the family was unhappy for his own personal reasons. Lady Sackville had never faced reality—and she had, Vita tells us, "an almost morbid shrinking from the facts of her own illegitimacy.[12] Lady Sackville loved Knole for its grandeur, its prestige; Lord Sackville loved it as a country squire loves his own land and the roots of a long heritage. To the young Vita, Knole meant even more: it was a living, organic symbol of England, the embodiment of everything English, and a part of her own being. Her love of it had a kind of Wordsworthian pantheistic quality:

It was different from one's love for any human being. It transcended it. I don't think my mother ever felt like that about Knole; not quite; not as my father did. She never got its values right; one could not have expected that of her. She was too Latin, somehow; too unreal; too fantastic altogether; too un-English. She exploited it. . . . Although she went wrong and got every possible value wrong and made my father and me clench our fists in silence whenever she talked about Knole, still, now I see that she contributed beauty to it in her own way.[13]

When Victoria's father won the case and the inheritance, the family made a triumphal procession back to Knole; and Vita had a few more years of the security of the ancestral estate. But in 1928, upon her father's death, a younger brother, Charles Sackville-West, succeeded him as Lord Sackville; and Charles' son became the sixth Baron Sackville in 1966.

III *Womanhood*

V. Sackville-West, an only child, was frightened of her mother; for she always felt that she had failed to fulfill her mother's ambition to have a "popular" daughter. With her father—a quiet, conscientious country gentleman—she felt more at ease; for both of them were unsociable and shared a distaste for weekend parties. But her childhood environment was also not an intellectual one; indeed, she turned to reading and writing in rebellion against the social code of her class. Victoria tells us that when she was twelve she read *Cyrano de Bergerac,* and she was so inspired that she started writing an enormous novel about Edward Sackville, fourth Earl of Dorset, who seemed the embodiment of romance to the young girl who was in love with the glamor of an ancient heritage. As V. Sackville-West says of herself at this time,

I never stopped after that,—historical novels, pretentious, quite uninteresting, pedantic, and all written at an unflagging speed: the day after one was finished, another would be begun. I think that between the ages of thirteen and nineteen I must have been quite dreadful. I was plain, priggish, studious (oh very!), totally uninspired, unmanageably and lankily tall—in fact, the only good thing that could be said of me was that I wouldn't have anything to do with my kind. Seeing that I was unpopular (and small wonder, for a saturnine prig), I wouldn't court popularity. I minded rather, and used to cry when I went to bed after coming home from a party, but I made myself defiant about it. I don't mean this to sound in the least pathetic; I wasn't unhappy, only solitary, but I don't pretend that I minded solitude, I rather chose it.[14]

This statement reveals the characteristics and temperament of the creative artist: the awareness of her ego, her sense of being different, her need for solitude. Furthermore, the adult Victoria remained basically unchanged—masculine, antisocial, defiant; but she fiercely loved literature, history, animals, the English countryside, and the architecture of fine houses.

In 1910, when she was eighteen, she "came out"—and she met Harold Nicolson. Fortunately, she says, her debut was a small, rather modest affair because of the recent death of Edward VII. "Thus," writes Victoria Sackville-West with her characteristic satirical turn of mind, "can the tragedies of great kings be turned to the uses of little people." During her debut season, and at a small dinner-and-theater party, she met her future husband; she was enamored by his youth, his charm, and his "aliveness." "What fun!" was the first remark she heard him make. "Everything was fun to his energy, vitality, and buoyancy. I liked his irrepressible brown curls, his laughing eyes, his charming smile, and his boyishness. But we didn't become particular friends. I think he looked upon me more of a child than I actually was, and as for myself I never thought about people, especially men, under a very pleasant aspect unless they made friendly advances to me first."[15]

But the friendship grew and turned into love during the year of 1911; and the young couple became secretly engaged; in October, 1913, they were quietly married in the chapel at Knole. After a honeymoon in Italy and Egypt, they went to Constantinople to live; for Harold Nicolson was employed there in the British Embassy. Victoria considered the next few years to be idyllic in every way. The two were deeply in love (as they remained throughout the marriage; indeed, their marriage seems to be becoming one of the great classic love-affairs of all time); and Victoria, during the early years of her marriage, was the compliant, loving wife, completely fulfilled:

The correct and adoring young wife of the brilliant diplomat came back to England in June, 1914. I remember a divine voyage by sea from Constantinople to Marseilles, through the Aegean, a second honeymoon. Then we went to Knole. War was declared on the fourth of August, and Ben was born on the sixth [her first child, Benedict]. We spent the winter in London and I became quite sociable. I was, in fact, thoroughly tamed. That was the only period of my life when I achieved anything like popularity. I was no longer plain, I took adequate trouble to make myself agreeable, Harold was loved by everyone who met him—we were, in fact, a nice young couple to ask out to dinner. Oh God, the horror of it.[16]

This passage from her autobiography is typical of Vita's objectivity—an almost masculine quality of mind—and of her ironic humor. The outbreak of World War I symbolized a turning point in Victoria Sackville-West's life; it was as if she suddenly ceased trying to be what she thought she ought to be—and began living her own life. She began writing in earnest, withdrew from the society of London, and spent much time in the country. The war also intensified the breach between her father and mother, and the two separated at the end of the war.

Since Harold Nicolson was exempted from war-service because of his work in the foreign office, the young couple remained together. They lived at 182 Ebury Street in Pimlico, or at Long Barn, a cottage they had bought at Sevenoaks-Weald, near Knole, in Kent: "In our personal life there was nothing except moving to London for the winter, to the cottage for the summer, watching Ben grow and learn to speak, and for me, writing. I should think it was hardly possible for two people to be more completely and unquestionably happy. There was never a cloud, never a squabble. I knew that if Harold died, I should die too; it all made life very simple. In the winter [January, 1917] Nigel [their second child] was born."[17]

Surely this marriage, as Nigel Nicolson says, was on the surface a strange one; either it would dissolve or become one of the finest relationships ever experienced by two extremely sensitive people. For husband and wife were totally different: Harold Nicolson was gay, outgoing, sociable, interested in politics and in the ways of the world; Victoria Sackville-West, mysterious, antisocial, undomesticated, interested in solitary pursuits—litera- ture and gardening. Nigel Nicolson tells us that only for a brief period in 1920 did the marriage seem to flounder, but it righted itself and even gathered strength after the momentary peril of shipwreck; from that point to the end, their concern for each other was the dominating factor of their lives. When apart they wrote to each other every day, from the time of their engagement in 1911 until Vita's death in 1962. Vita, however, was not a good letter writer—and the apparent "dullness" of her life led her to excuse the shortness of her letters with the phrase, "another great day at Sissinghurst"—a phrase which became a family joke. Such letters she labelled "village" letters[18]

For the most part Vita remained at Long Barn, writing, gardening, and remodeling the house, while her husband traveled to his foreign posts. Her first book—a three-act drama on the life of Thomas Chatterton—had been privately printed in 1909, when Victoria Sackville-West was seventeen. But in 1917 her first genuine work was published, *Poems of West and East*. With this publication V. Sackville-West, poet and novelist, emerged; for she was now fully aware of her purpose in life, confident in a new power of artistic insight, and sure of her facility in the craft of writing. In 1917, at twenty-five, her personality burst into full bloom. In her masculinity, she detested the name Victoria and wanted recognition not as a *woman*-poet (whenever a reviewer referred to her as a "poetess" or "auth- oress," she clenched her fists in rage), and so she devised the signature "V. Sackville-West," which she used for the rest of her life.

There are many reasons, and complexities, that contributed to the birth of V. Sackville-West as a novelist and poet. First of all, marriage and World War I freed her from parental control and the shackles of "Society." Ill-at-ease with most people of her class and in rebellion against the round of social duties demanded of a young aristocratic "lady" of the Edwardian period, she found her own life in the new freedom of London, in the Kentish countryside, in her husband's understanding, and in the companionship of members of the "Bloomsbury Group." Although Harold Nicolson differed from his wife in being, on the whole, a conformist, he was a sensitive person; his aristocracy, an intellectual one; his interest, humane. Certainly, at least in the early years of their married life, his influence upon Vita was considerable. He drew her out; he appreciated her fineness, and encouraged her writing. Perhaps the greatest proof of Harold Nicolson's appreciation of his wife is that he finally gave up a diplomatic career and turned to writing and a journalist's life so that the two of them could be together and share more fully the inner life. An entry in his diary best explains what these two persons came to mean to each other:

Going up in the train I think what it is that makes us so indispensable to each other. I think it is this. (a) That we each respect in the other some central core of reality. (b) Neither of us would find it easy to define that core, but we are aware of it and the other know [sic] that it is there and recognized. This produces a feeling of not having to strive or posture. It is not a question of sincerity or insincerity. It is merely that when with each other we relax completely. Thus we get the maximum satisfaction out of a static relationship. (c) Yet our relations are also dynamic. We stimulate each other. We are not merely intellectual chairs to each other, we are intellectual exercise. I think it is the perfect adjustment between these two elements, the static and the dynamic, which creates such harmony in our lives. No one else knows or understands. Oh my precious, my gentle, my magnificent Vita![19]

Vita also depicted what the marriage meant to her in a letter that she wrote in June, 1929, just after she had parted from her husband at a London railroad station when he was returning to his diplomatic post in Berlin:

What is so torturing when I leave you at these London stations and drive off is the knowledge that you are still there—that, for half an hour or three-quarters of an hour, I could still return and find you; come up behind you, take you by the elbow, and say "Hadji."

I came straight home, feeling horribly desolate and sad, driving down that familiar and dreary road. I remembered Rasht and our parting there; our parting at Victoria when you left for Persia; till our life seemed made up of partings, and I wondered how long it would continue.

Then I came round the corner on to the view—our view—and I thought how you loved it, and how simple you were, really, apart from our activity; and how I loved you for being both simple and active in one and the same person.

Then I came home, and it was no consolation at all. You see, when I am unhappy for other reasons, the cottage is a real solace to me; but when it is on account of you that I am unhappy (because you have gone away) it is an additional pang—it is the same place, but a sort of mockery and emptiness hangs about it—I almost wish that just once you could lose me and then come straight back to the cottage and find it still full of me but empty of me, then you would know what I go through after you have gone away.

Anyhow, you will say, it is worse for you who go back to a horrible and alien city, whereas I stay in the place we both love so much; but really, Hadji, it is no consolation to come back to a place full of coffee-cups—there was a cardboard box lid, full of your rose-petals, still on the terrace.

You are dearer to me than anybody ever has been or ever could be. If you died suddenly, I should kill myself as soon as I had made provision for the boys. I really mean this. I could not live if I lost you. I do not think one could conceive of a love more exclusive, more tender, or more pure than I have for you. I think it is immortal, a thing which happens seldom.

Darling, there are not many people who would write such a letter after sixteen years of marriage, yet who would be saying therein only one-fiftieth of what they were feeling as they wrote it. I sometimes try to tell you the truth, and then I find that I have no words at my command which could possibly convey it to you.[20]

Vita was not usually so voluble in her letters: apparently, she found it more difficult than did her husband to reveal herself. Her son Nigel admits that others knew her better, more intimately, than did members of her family, who often declared that they did not know what she was thinking until they had opened her latest book. The greatest intimacy of the marriage seemed to have grown, in part, from their mutual love for Sissinghurst, the ruined old tower which had belonged to the

Sackvilles in the sixteenth century, and which the Nicolsons purchased (as a consolation prize for the loss of Knole?) in 1930. At this time, too, Vita renounced the allowance from her mother (which was Vita's legal right) so that the Nicolsons lived from hand-to-mouth, or rather from book-to-book. Both husband and wife intensely enjoyed rebuilding the tower, the cottages, and the garden of this estate. Nigel writes that, when his parents were by themselves, they did not talk of profundities but of the ordinary events—about the garden, domestic affairs, the dogs, and the tenants.

We must conclude that this marriage, certainly a very happy one, nevertheless meant more to the husband than to the wife. Although Vita liked the *fact* of marriage, she detested it as an institution. She never introduced Sir Harold as "my husband," she disliked "anniversaries" and all of the usual domestic rituals, and she was not possessive in familial relationships. In times of stress, she grew hard—he, soft. And we suspect that Sir Harold had to do more than half of the adjusting, if we accept the following entry in his diary:

I have got into the way of taking my happiness for granted. Yet Viti [*sic*] is not a person one can take for granted. She is a dark river moving deeply in shadows. She really does not care for domestic affections. She would wish life to be conducted on a series of *grandes passions*. Or she thinks she would. In practice had I been a passionate man, I should have suffered tortures of jealousy on her behalf, have made endless scenes, and we should now have separated.[21]

One final quotation from the letters of Sir Harold Nicolson completes the picture of their married life:

Why did you ask me whether I was happy in life? You asked it in such an odd way. I mean I felt that you imagined I was not happy . . . I love my life nowadays more than I have ever loved it. For what, after all, is happiness? Occupation in congenial surroundings? . . . You know how I love the House and what warm friends I have there. But behind the House there is my own life. There are the boys, who mean a great deal to me. There are my friends. And there is you, my dearest—and about that I think that your dear muddle-head gets confused. You believe so much in passion that you under-estimate love. I know that the central thing in myself (the actual main-spring which makes all the little cogs go round and round so busily) is my love for you. It is the rock on which my life is founded.

I know it bores you to realize that we are married—and, by the way, we shall shortly have a silver wedding. You must admit that I have always respected that side in your eccentricity. But whatever you may feel about it, the fact remains that you are the only person whom I shall want to be with me were I in pain. Oh my dearest Vita, I love you so. And as we both know this fact, we evade it. It is the silent secret between ourselves.[22]

Of one fact we may be certain: after the first few years of married life, the freedom, the sense of security, and the companionship of her husband enabled V. Sackville-West to blossom. She emerged a free spirit, self-confident, and convinced of the powers of her artistry. Without any hesitation, she embarked seriously and earnestly upon her career; and in it she found complete fulfillment.

IV *Maturity*

V. Sackville-West's first important novel was *Heritage* (1919), a work that drew the attention of influential critics and established her reputation as a novelist. Then came her long poem *The Land* (1929) which won for her the coveted Hawthornden Prize. In swift succession she wrote *The Edwardians* (1930), which was a book-of-the-month club selection; *All Passion Spent* (perhaps her finest novel); and *Family History*. This period from 1926 to 1938, the beginning of World War II, was her most fecund one.

Almost constantly at work, she found herself becoming famous. As soon as one book was off the press, she went to work upon another. By this time Sir Harold had given up his diplomatic career and was also busily writing, and their life flowed easily at Sissinghurst, where the restoration of the house and the creation of the gardens filled almost every moment of the time spared from their writing. Vita was broadcasting over the British Broadcasting Company and writing for *Action*, a new liberal paper edited by Sir Harold. Although this journal lasted only about a year, it was a significant part of the liberal movement; and it enhanced Sir Harold's reputation as a journalist and as a spokesman for the New Voice of England.

In January, 1933, the Nicolsons undertook an American lecture tour which lasted for three months. At this time they were better known in the United States than in Britain; and the American public fell in love with Vita. Sometimes the two lectured together, sometimes separately. She was called "Juno-esque"; "Portia-like"; "Orlando." And the "V." was variously interpreted as Virginia or Vera. In Des Moines, Iowa, it was reported that "the Countess Vera Sackville-West spoke to an attentive audience for almost twenty minutes. Then she suddenly stopped, dropped her head and quietly said, "I have forgotten what I was going to say." For this lapse, the audience loved her. Another paper reported that "she has the glorious rosy skin that bespeaks more chapters written under the drifting petals of her apple-orchard at Long Barn, Kent, than in a leather-scented library."[23]

The Americans not only adored her but liked her clothes (the kind of clothes, Sir Harold once remarked, that Beatrice would have worn had she married Dante) and respected her quiet dignity. Vita lectured again and again in Boston, Chicago, St. Louis, Cincinnati, Kansas City, Newark, Montreal, and Los Angeles. But, except for Niagara Falls and the Grand Canyon, the Nicolsons hated America—especially the endless procession of teas, dinners, and receptions.

When Vita saw Niagara Falls on January 31, 1933, she wrote enthusiastically to her husband:

Niagara is really some waterfall! It falls over like a great noisy beard made of cotton-wool, veiled by spray and spanned by rainbows. The rainbows are the most unexpected part of it. They stand across like bridges between America and Canada, and are reproduced in sections among the boiling foam. The spray rises to the height of a skyscraper shot by sudden iridescence high up in the air. There is a strange and impressive alliance between the works of God and the works of man. . . . I think it is very good for you and me to have come to America. I am glad we did. I am getting a lot out of it. There may be moments when we are tired and nauseated and bored. But on the whole it is infinitely valuable.[24]

Her feeling for the Grand Canyon found expression in a novel of that name; and, in the discussion of the work, we shall see how the novelist in her utilized that experience. In November, 1933, *Collected Poems* was published. Next came *The Dark Island,* a strange and desolate novel, which most of the critics found "morbid and distressing."[25] Sir Harold did not like it, either. In 1935, Vita was working on her biography of Joan of Arc—a piece for which she did a thorough job of research which utilized her excellent command of French. Then she wrote *Pepita*, the story of her grandmother and grandfather. Between books, she enjoyed trips to France, Italy, Morocco, Algeria.

But more importantly was the progress of remodeling at Sissinghurst. With the death of her mother in 1936, Vita inherited a small fortune, most of which was spent rebuilding Sissinghurst. In June, 1937, Sir Harold wrote to his wife:

Never has Sissinghurst looked more lovely or been more appreciated. . . . You with your extraordinary taste have made it like nobody's garden but your own. I think the secret of your gardening is simply that you have the courage to abolish ugly or unsuccessful flowers. Except for those beastly red-hot pokers which you have a weakness for, there is not an ugly flower in the whole place. Then I think *si j'ose m'exprimer ainsi*, that the design is really good. I mean we have got what we wanted to get—a perfect proportion between the classic and the romantic, between the element of expectation and the element of surprise. Thus the main axes are terminated in a way to satisfy expectation, yet they are in themselves so tricky that they also cause surprise. But the point of the garden will not be apparent until the hedges have grown up, especially (most important of all) the holly hedge in the flower garden. But it is lovely, lovely, lovely—and you must be pleased with your work.[26]

And when, in October, 1937, Vita was on a motor trip in France, Sir Harold wrote: "And do you realize, my dearest Viti, (bless you) how much it means that we should each of us be as excited about Sissinghurst and feel that we have a chance there which is an enormous chance. I really believe that you will be able to make of that ramshackle farm-tumble something as personal and lovely as anything in England. I confess that I am deeply impressed by your fore-sight or vision in such matters. . . . I think it was your poem that made me realize about Sissing-hurst first."[27]

By 1938, the idyllic country life was shattered. To both of them—but especially to Sir Harold, for Vita hated politics and never understood them—the imminency of war was apparent. While Sir Harold was in London and involved in the Munich crisis, Vita stayed at Sissinghurst. In September, she wrote that preparations of war were being carried out as if it were a fact; and she also evinced her awareness of her "Englishness":

Everyone is calm, resolute and cheerful. One hears more jokes than ever, although they all realize quite well what it means. I do respect the English, for all their faults! I do not know whether you have found the same psychological experience going on in yourself as I am finding during these dreadful days: a sort of strange calm and resignation, a mood which scarcely fluctuates at all save in brief moments of human weakness. I feel almost exalted, and most strangely part of a corporate body called England, and not merely "England," but of all whose ideals and principles are at this moment similar ... I might put it like this: that the strings of one's being are tuned up to their finest pitch.[28]

During the war, Vita and Sir Harold did much broadcasting and writing; and each carried a small vial of poison to take if England lost and life became unbearable. One other small incident from their lives illustrates their attitudes at this time. In November, 1938, Sir Harold was invited to attend a banquet at Buckingham Palace in honor of the King of Romania. Vita, who had promised to accompany him, declined at the last minute because she could not bring herself to spend the money necessary for the proper dress and accessories; and she wrote to her husband: "I am writing this letter with my jewels littered all around me—emeralds and diamonds, just taken out of the bank—and they make me feel sick; I simply can't subscribe any longer to the world which these jewels represent. I can't buy a dress costing £30 or wear jewels worth £2,000 when people are starving. I can't support such a farce when people are threatened that their electric light or gas may be cut off because they can't pay their arrears."[29] To this letter her husband replied:

How I do love you, Mar! I am glad you are not coming. You are quite right as usual. It is wrong to spend all that money merely to go to a party. That sort of world is dead today. How can a person of your sensitiveness and imagination doll yourself up in expensive clothes when there are cultured Jewish women and men hiding like foxes in the Grunewald? My God! I do admire you so, Viti. You are so sound in your values. They ring like a bell. It makes me feel so confident that if I ever strike that bell, it always echoes the perfect note. I shall never forget what you meant to me during the crisis [the Munich crisis]. You were all that were spiritually perfect during those days. I could not have stood them had you not been there as a sort of completely selfless person, right above all the petty fears and jangles.[30]

About six months later Sir Harold, when he wrote again to Vita, was in despair about England's future. This passage well displays not only Sir Harold's feelings but Vita's also:

Dearest, why can we not be left alone? We are doing no harm. We care for fine and gentle things. We wish only to do good on earth. We are not vulgar in our tastes or cruel in our thoughts. Why is it that we are impotent to prevent something which we know to be evil and terrible? I would willingly give my own life if I could stop this war. I would go round to the doctor and be put out of this world without a pang. Yet I cannot think enough to stop it. What a little thing my head is, and what a great thing is hatred when unlocked. I am so unhappy about the outside, and so happy in my own little orbit.[31]

In 1939 Vita, who had no new book in the writing, was engaged in writing articles for the *New Statesman* on gardening and in broadcasting. During the war years, she wrote mostly nonfiction—articles about the English and about various aspects of English life. As is natural, the national spirit flourishes in wartime; and V. Sackville-West's feeling for things British, for the good things in English life, was uppermost in her thoughts.

One novel, published in 1942, is a war novel, *Grand Canyon*. Although the setting is American, it is a poignant story of the dying gasps of the human race—what Vita feared would happen if England were to be destroyed by Hitler. The 1940's also saw the publication of *The Eagle and the Dove*: a biographical study of two saints—St. Teresa of Ávila and Ste. Thérèse of Lisieux. This work, which demanded much time and research, is a shining tour de force and was at once so acclaimed.

The 1950's witnessed the culmination of her career; for, recognized now as one of England's leading writers, V. Sackville-West became the recipient of many honors. As Fellow of the Royal Society of Literature, she wrote and read scholarly papers on Andrew Marvell, Mrs. Aphra Behn, Walter de la Mare, and others; and the *Daughter of France*, which appeared in 1959, is an erudite biography of Anne Marie d'Orléans, Duchess of Montpensier (1627-1693). Oxford University bestowed upon

V. Sackville-West a D. Litt., and she was made Companion of
Honor in 1958. Her family life was replete with happiness;
Sissinghurst became one of the showplaces in England.

She died in 1962 at the age of seventy; and until near the
end, she was producing; indeed, her last novel, *No Signposts
in the Sea,* was published only a year before her death. Surely
no woman ever had a richer life or was more completely fulfilled:
in her writing career she had achieved success and recognition;
she was deeply cherished by a devoted and charming husband;
she had two fine sons, each recognized in his own field. We
might well recall the lines from Milton's *Samson Agonistes,*
which she herself quoted at the opening of *All Passion Spent*:

> All is best, though we oft doubt,
> What th' unsearchable dispose
> Of highest wisdom brings about,
> And ever best found in the close . . .
> . . . .
> His servants he with new acquist
> Of true experience from this great event
> With peace and consolation hath dismist,
> And calm of mind all passion spent.[32]

CHAPTER 2

Orlando: *Friendship with Virginia Woolf and the Bloomsbury Group*

> "And though she had a great gift for a few
> very intimate friendships, like that with Vir-
> ginia Woolf, she found mere acquaintance
> difficult."   —Sir Harold Nicolson[1]

I *The Bloomsbury Group*

WHEN V. Sackville-West and Harold Nicolson returned
to England from the Near East after their first few years
of marriage, they took an apartment on Ebury Street in the Pimlico district of London and became neighbors of George Moore,
one of the leaders of the Bloomsbury Group. He was instrumen-
tal in getting V. Sackville-West's first book, *Heritage,* published
in 1919, a date that seems to be about right for the beginning
of the Nicolsons' contact with the Bloomsbury Group; for in
a letter to her husband, V. Sackville-West wrote that it would
perhaps have been better if they had known the Bloomsbury
Group in 1916 instead of remaining with the Edwardian world.
But, she said, they never even knew of the existence of this
group in 1916.[2] So it may safely be assumed that the Nicolsons
became acquainted with the group about 1919 or 1920.[3] How
great the influence of this group was upon the work of V. Sackville-West and just what the nature of this influence was are
somewhat difficult to ascertain.

Even now little is known about the so-called "Bloomsbury
Group." It seems always to have been simply a gathering of close
friends: in no sense was it an organized movement, for it had
no creeds, no common cause. About 1906 these people began
meeting at the home of Virginia and Vanessa Stephen, daughters
of Leslie Stephen, who lived in the Bloomsbury district of London. (Virginia became the wife of Leonard Woolf, and Vanessa

32

married Clive Bell.) The title of the Group was first used derisively; and the label "Bloomsberries" was coined by Desmond MacCarthy's wife. Writers, artists, and philosophers drifted in and out of the Group, but a few formed the core. Some of these, besides the Nicolsons and the Woolfs, were E. M. Forster, Lytton Strachey, Desmond MacCarthy, Maynard Keynes, Roger Fry, Clive Bell, Violet Trefusis, Lord Lascelles, and George Moore.[4]

These and others came together of an evening to discuss ideas and concepts which seemed to them vital issues facing the contemporary artist. Some of these ideas are expressed in George Moore's *Principia Ethica*. First, in the esthetics of the Bloomsbury philosophy, there was more than a touch of mysticism. Love in its many aspects is the only faith that matters; it embraces and sublimates all of life's experiences. Therefore, personal relationships are of the utmost importance, and love becomes the universal mystique. E. M. Forster, for example, stressed in many of his works (notably *A Passage to India*) the idea that only mystic contemplation can make any sense out of life. Panic, fear, emptiness, the "aloneness" of the individual—these are the enemies born of society that threaten the splendor of life.

The second principle in Moore's philosophy is the power of the intellect. It must solve the complicated problems of life; and, although it cannot by itself create a work of art, it must organize the raw materials. Literature, like painting, stated Moore in the *Principia*, is not an imitation of the external world; it is not representational. Roger Fry (artist and art critic, 1866-1934) applied this principle when he wrote that the permanent levels in literature depict a closely organized life; that they present inexorable laws, such as cause and effect; that they show a fate indifferent to human desires but working toward an inevitable conclusion.[5] In sum, a work of art must be selective, closely structured; it cannot rely upon chance, which is more readily acceptable in life than in fiction. (What appears to the reader to be chance in Thomas Hardy's novels—an appearance which lends to them an air of reality—is actually an artifice in a tightly structured plot.) Literature has its own laws, its own truths, and its own functions.

Third, and most important in the development of the novel, is the role of the subconscious in a work of art, a matter of

special concern to the "Bloomsberries." Since the early 1920's
was the Golden Age of psychology, of the dissemination of the
theories of Sigmund Freud, Carl Jung, Otto Rank, and Alfred
Adler, it is not surprising to find the principles of psychology
and psychoanalysis contributing greatly to the form and content of the novel. The result, of course, was the birth of the
"stream-of-consciousness" novel in England, as created by
James Joyce and Virginia Woolf. Obviously, to the "Bloomsberries" a novel is held together not by a string of events but
by a connection of emotions, by the unfolding of one emotion,
or by the creation of a mood. The core of the novel becomes
the portrayal of a personality, of the inner life of a character.

This final concept is particularly important in a reading of
V. Sackville-West's fiction. She was never primarily concerned
with plot; she was interested in action only as it helped to
uncover or reveal emotions. Much of the criticism which was
expressed upon the publication of her novels was directed at
a lack of tight structure and of character-development, but this
criticism becomes somewhat irrelevant when we consider this
outstanding characteristic—the communication of an emotion
with all its tensions, implications, effects, and manifestations.

The esthetic creed of the Bloomsbury Group, formulated by
Moore, was most explicitly and artistically implemented by
Virginia Woolf; however, V. Sackville-West was a close second.
The two women, as we shall soon see, held many of the same
basic concepts of art and life. Temperamentally, V. Sackville-
West was at home with the "Bloomsberries." It was not so much
that she learned their code or that they exerted any specific
influence; they merely voiced her own thoughts and feelings,
her own instincts concerning artistic matters and the esthetics
of creativity. As she herself stated in *Joan of Arc,* she trusted
her instinct to cut through to the truth, to the "real" wisdom,
more than she did her intellect.[6] And yet she could organize
and order her ideas logically with a power almost masculine.
It was, in fact, this ability which Virginia Woolf most admired
in her friend.

The philosophic statement of George Moore does seem to
have impressed V. Sackville-West, and E. M. Forster's novels
may have suggested some ideas and techniques. Two qualities
of E. M. Forster's writings which she must have found espe-

cially congenial were his mysticism and his feeling for the English countryside. Moore's influence seems to appear in her emphasis upon the supremacy of love, the need for "selectivity" in art, the reality of the "inner life," the application of the theory of the subconscious in characterization.

In the late 1930's the Bloomsbury Group began to disintegrate. No doubt, with the changing times, the threat of war, and the rise of Naziism, the interests of the members of the Group shifted; and matters other than art became preeminent. But, as the Group declined, it began to acquire a "bad name." In a letter to Sir Harold, dated November 15, 1938, V. Sackville-West expressed her own theory about this loss of prestige: "How wrong people are about Bloomsbury, saying that it is devitalised and devitalising. You couldn't find two people less devitalised or devitalising than the Wolves [Woolfs]—or indeed people more vitalising than Roger Fry for example. I think where Bloomsbury has suffered is in its hangers-on like —— and equivalent young men, and of course the drooping Lytton [Lytton Strachey, writer: 1880-1932] must have done its cause a great harm. I hated Lytton."[7] Whatever the reason for the dissolution of the Group, it had served its purpose and had done its work. The members who were still alive and active during the war years had other work to do; furthermore, they had long been established writers—functioning independently and developing their own particular talents in their own areas.

II Orlando: *Friendship with Virginia Woolf*

It is no exaggeration to say that V. Sackville-West's best friend—and perhaps her only intimate one—was Virginia Woolf, who indeed amply returned the affection. Although the two met in 1922,[8] probably through the Bloomsbury Group, they did not become fast friends until 1924. But the relationship was a complicated one, as it was bound to be, because of the artistic sensibilities and complexities of these two women. On the surface, it appears that they had much in common: their writing careers, their staunch feminism, their rejection of the social changes of their time, and their isolation or escape into their own inner worlds. But these two artistic individuals also complemented each other as opposites; for as Jean Guiguet in her *Virginia Woolf and Her Works* has expressed it, "Virginia Woolf found in her friend qualities that she herself lacked but greatly admired—vigor, robustness, and unself-consciousness—qualities that her own fragility and introspection made impossible."[9] Meanwhile, V. Sackville-West found in Virginia Woolf the fire of genius, a sparkling and creative mind, a quick wit, and a greatness in her attitude towards life that made everyone of her visits a source of inspiration. Nigel Nicolson speaks of this electric quality of Virginia Woolf's: "I remember above all the visits from and to Virginia Woolf at the period when *Orlando* was in crucible, visits that even to a child were full of drama."[10]

As the friendship deepened, the two couples were often together. V. Sackville-West spoke with much affection of Leonard Woolf—of his boyishness, his enthusiasm, his essential simplicity. Surely the characters Viola and Leonard Anquetil in *The Edwardians* and in *Family History* are based upon the "Wolves"; upon these fictional characters V. Sackville-West bestowed the qualities she most admired in her friends: freedom from the routine of life, emphasis upon ideas and art, nonconformity in society.

During the summer of 1926, while Virginia Woolf was writing *To the Lighthouse*, she saw a great deal of V. Sackville-West.[11] She also did so the following summer, and it was then that the idea of writing *Orlando* occurred to her. The chief character, Orlando, is, of course, V. Sackville-West; around her are grouped all of Virginia Woolf's friends, who are more or less distinguished.[12] In the words of Frank Baldanza, the purpose of *Orlando* is "to explore the complexities of selfhood, of time, and of sexual differences through material provided by Mrs. Woolf's idea of her friend 'Vita.' "[13] Part of the material in *Orlando* is the history of the Sackvilles and of Knole.

Orlando was to Virginia Woolf a kind of joke, a *tour de force*. First came the amusing idea of manipulating time—the novel begins about 1570, when Orlando is a sixteen-year-old Elizabethan nobleman; at the end of the novel, it is 1928, and Orlando is thirty-six (the correct age for Vita). The idea for the change of sex occurred to Virginia Woolf when she saw a resemblance between V. Sackville-West and the Honourable Edward Sackville (whose portrait by Cornelius Nuie serves as a frontispiece to the first edition of *Orlando*), and she wished to depict the combination she had found in her friend of the courage of a man and the grace of a woman. Amused by these fantastic ideas, Virginia Woolf started work on the novel in October, 1927; and she gave herself a week to write this masquerade. But the idea ballooned, and the book was not finished until March, 1928. During the time of composition, the two women were much together; there were trips to Knole to choose pictures and to "get the feel" of the continuity of time of the entire Sackville tradition which meant so much to V. Sackville-West.

To understand *Orlando*, the reader most not take it seriously; he must laugh at the exaggerations, the incongruities, and especially he must be able to relish the author's sense of humor. Everything is so much in the spirit of fun that the reader should be able to laugh with Virginia Woolf at the gentle satire. For instance, Orlando takes to writing and fancies himself the author of a great English epic, which he carries with him always—through four centuries! Orlando has two faults: his compulsion to write and his love of nature (the universal English weakness). Of his *penchant* for literature, Mrs. Woolf wrote: "Let him leave books, they said, to the palsied or the dying. But worse was to come. For once the disease of reading has laid hold upon the system it weakens it so that it falls an easy prey to that other scourge which dwells in the ink pot and festers in the quill, the wretch takes to writing."[14] Her satire here is ironic, in the Swiftian tradition; and we understand that she is only teasing her friend, V. Sackville-West.

The other affliction, love of nature, which Virginia Woolf called "the English disease,"[15] is one from which her friend also suffered. Orlando is forever working at his agrarian epic, *The Oak Tree*; and the few lines of Orlando's poem that are quoted were taken from V. Sackville-West's *The Land*. Obviously the oak tree is a symbol, for in *Orlando* it is not only a poem but also a real tree. Virginia Woolf seems to be saying that nature and art are one in her friend; V. Sackville-West's inspiration, her artistic impulse, stems from nature—from her awareness of her long heritage of English culture. Near the end of the novel, Mrs. Woolf shows a tender understanding of what the loss of Knole meant to V. Sackville-West when Orlando sighs and thinks to himself: "The house was no longer hers... it belongs to time now; to history; was past the touch and control of the living."[16]

Another example of Mrs. Woolf's satire in *Orlando* is found in her summary of English literary history and criticism through the figure of Nick Greene, who courses through the four centuries with almost as many changes and transfigurations as Orlando. Surely unscrupulous Nick Greene, Elizabethan gossip columnist, was suggested by Robert Greene and by his attack upon Shakespeare in *A Groatsworth of Wit*. Greene is invited to visit Orlando; lives, as long as he can, off the bounty of his wealthy patron (who pathetically keeps asking him to read *The Oak Tree*); and then turns around and writes a devastating satire about Orlando. Professor Baldanza has pointed out the similarity of this situation to that used by Roy Campbell in his poem *The Georgiad* (1933) to satirize most cruelly the Bloomsbury Group, especially the Nicolsons and Virginia Woolf.[17]

In *Orlando*, Virginia Woolf tries to point out the many diverse strains in our personalities resulting from inheritances, the many diverse different selves within each of us. She was much interested in lesbianism; and perhaps aware of her own dual makeup, she once said that "in every human being a vacillation from one sex to the other takes place, and often it is only the clothes that keep the male or female likeness, while underneath the sex is the very opposite of what it is above."[18] Not only do all of us have many selves, we also have many forms of love.

With *Orlando* finished, V. Sackville-West and Virginia Woolf took a vacation trip to France; and the friendship seemed to deepen. Upon hearing of her friend's suicide on March 31, 1941, V. Sackville-West was grievously hurt; her letter to her husband about the death expresses not only sorrow but incredulity that such a vital person could be dead, and anger at a world that made such a tragedy possible. The finest tribute, however, that V. Sackville-West paid her friend is in an account of a visit made to the Woolfs' house on August 3, 1938. This extract is from a letter to Sir Harold. "We sat out in the garden watching the late sunlight making the corn golden over the Downs. Then I had a long talk this morning with Virginia, who was in her most delightful mood. . . . Oh, my dear, what an enchanting person Virginia is! How she weaves magic into life! Whenever I see her, she raises life to a higher level."[19] Certain it is that these two influences, contact with the Bloomsbury Group and especially her friendship with Virginia Woolf, helped greatly to mature the artist in V. Sackville-West.

CHAPTER 3

Biographer and Historian

> "Few tasks of the historian or biographer can be more misleading than the reconstruction of a forgotten character . . ."
>
> —V. Sackville-West[1]

M ISS SACKVILLE-WEST wrote much in genres other than the novel and poetry; in fact, because there is hardly a literary genre she did not employ, we are amazed at the versatility and diversity of her writing. She wrote numerous essays about the British countryside and about gardening; she recorded her travels in the Near East in two important travel books; she wrote a biographical history about her ancestors and Knole; she explored literary history in her scholarly essays about Andrew Marvell, Aphra Behn, and Walter de la Mare; and she wrote four biographies which took solid research work and which recreate the eras involved. Because of the great amount of the work she produced, we have space only to glance at her most significant writing in biographical and historical areas.

I The Travel Books

The subject of Miss Sackville-West's two travel books was unusual for the 1920's since not many people had traveled widely in the Near East, especially Persia. It is not remarkable that Sir Harold Nicolson was especially fond of these works since he had spent several years in Persia in the British consular service and since the two of them had explored much of this section of the world together. The first of the two books, *Passenger to Teheran* (1926), is dedicated to Sir Harold. The arm-chair traveler visits, with Miss Sackville-West, Egypt, Iraq, Persia (including Teheran and Isfahan), Kum, and Russia. In the second book, *Twelve Days: An Account of a Journey Across*

the Bakhtari Mountains in Southwestern Persia (1928), the
reader crosses rugged, desert land to Yezd-i-khast and to Shalam-
zar before he begins his mountainous climb. Both books are
remarkable for the descriptions of villages, of the natives, and
of life in these countries. But, for most readers today, the chief
attraction is the personal and subjective points of views that
the author expresses: the "asides." For instance, as Miss Sackville-
West admires a natural scene, she wonders whether nature,
rather than human nature, has a greater power to move and
excite—and, if nature does, is the result a good traveler but a
poor, and inadequate, friend?[2]

Generally, her fine writing, her gift of the exact word or
phrase, and her precise clarity are especially evident in her
prose. Her style is simple, always lucid; and her point of view
is especially English. This English quality is found in her articles
on English country houses and on English outdoor life—articles
that present to us neat comments on the English temperament—
ideas which were very much a part of her and her life. Her
sentiments, her love of England, her thorough understanding of
the country—and of the English people—all these lay close to her
heart. She was in love with England (much as Joan of Arc was
in love with France), and she could wax poetic in expressing
this feeling: "England is green throughout; her seas, her woods,
her fields all island-green. Green, quiet England."[3]

To Sackville-West, England meant rural England; and the
English people meant the country gentry and the workers of
the land. Industrialism remained to her a mortal enemy that
blackened everything it touched; and urban life was equally
distasteful to her. For this reason, she found rural domestic
architecture better than the urban: "There is nothing quite like
the English country house anywhere else in the world."[4] Such
a house is not only *in* the country; it is part of it. For this reason,
as well as for personal reasons, she loved Knole and Sissinghurst.

II Knole and the Sackvilles

In her history *Knole and the Sackvilles,* Sackville-West tells
the history of a family as represented and preserved by a house.
Knole, the ancient home of the Sackvilles, is truly one of the
most beautiful monuments of English architecture. Not so

pretentious as Blenheim or so stately as Longleat, it is magnificent but also warm and gracious. There is nothing of the
nouveau riche about it. Sackville-West describes the view as
the visitor approaches the estate: "One looks down upon this
house from a certain corner in the garden . . . the house lies
below one in the hollow, lovely in its colour and its serenity.
It has all the quality of peace and permanence; of mellow age;
of stateliness and tradition. It is gentle and venerable. Yet it is,
as I have said, gay. It has the deep inward gaiety of some very
old woman who has always been beautiful. It is, above all, an
English house. It has the tone of England. . . .[5]

After the opening description of the house, Miss Sackville-
West turns to its history. The oldest portions of Knole date back
to the time of Bourchier, the Archbishop of Canterbury, who
bought the house in 1456. Cardinal Morton, too, lived in it;
and we wonder whether Thomas More, as a boy, served here
his apprenticeship to Morton. When Cranmer became Archbishop, Henry VIII expressed a liking for Knole; and the Archbishop diplomatically handed it over to the Crown. It then
passed through the hands of various court favorites until Queen
Elizabeth in 1586 gave it to her cousin Thomas Sackville. It
remained in the Sackville family until recently, when it became
one of the National Trust Estates.

Of her own ancestors Victoria Sackville-West writes that their
interest for her lies in the fact that they were representatives
of their times; but for us there is an added interest: their significance in the literary history of England and the importance of
the family tradition to Sackville-West. The first chapter introduces us to the first Earl of Dorset, Thomas Sackville, who
loomed large in the annals of England, both historical and
literary. He had a long life (1536-1608) and flourished under
the reigns of both Queen Elizabeth and James I, becoming, in
1603, Lord Treasurer of the realm. Miss Sackville-West, who
believes that he gave up a first-rate literary career to become a
second-rate politician, underrates his diplomatic success; after
all, he lived to become one of the three most influential men
in the realm.

The next chapter presents a picture of life at Knole during
the days of Richard Sackville, the third Earl of Dorset (1589-
1624) whose wife was Lady Anne Clifford. This chapter is

lively and vivid because Lady Anne left a diary which was edited
by Miss Sackville-West and published in 1923. The diary makes
no pretence at being literary; it is full of the everyday matters
of life—her dresses, the illnesses of her child, the cooking, and
the affairs of the servants. But it gives us a realistic picture of
everyday life of its time; and it makes good reading, as V.
Sackville-West has edited it.

The fourth Earl of Dorset (the subject of Chapter Five) was
to V. Sackville-West the embodiment of the Cavalier in the
reign of Charles I. At thirteen, Victoria wrote, as we have noted,
a lengthy novel about him and his two sons. As Sackville-West
portrays him in *Knole,* he is a romantic figure: a handsome
young man, he was devoted to King Charles; had fought a duel
with Lord Bruce; had acquired from the king the East Coast
of America from Boston to New York (along with the islands
nearby—Long Island, Sandy Hook, Block Island, Martha's Vineyard, and others); and had played an active role in the war
against Cromwell. When Knole itself was captured by the
Roundheads, the Earl's two sons were taken prisoners; and the
younger one was murdered by a Roundhead soldier. After the
execution of the king, the Earl vowed that he would never
again stir out of his house until carried out in his coffin—a vow
he kept.

Knole in the Restoration became a gay place; for Charles,
the sixth Earl, was a high-living, pleasure-loving cavalier.
Thomas Macaulay's portrait of him V. Sackville-West believes
to be a judicious evaluation (except for the fact that Dorset's
poetry is overevaluated):

Such a patron of letters England had never seen. This bounty was
bestowed with equal judgment and liberality, and was confined
to no sect or faction. . . . Dryden owned that he had been saved
from ruin by Dorset's princely generosity. Yet Montague and Prior,
who had keenly satirized Dryden, were introduced by Dorset into
public life; and the best comedy of Dryden's mortal enemy, Shadwell,
was written at Dorset's country seat. The munificent Earl might, if
such had been his wish, have been the rival of those of whom he
was content to be the benefactor. For the verses which he occasionally
composed, unstudied as they are, exhibit the traces of genius which,
assiduously cultivated, would have produced something great.[6]

Miss Sackville-West relates an amusing anecdote about a "literary" party at Knole. At this time, Dryden, who was a constant visitor, was an honored guest at a party at which someone proposed that each guest write an impromptu verse and the poet-laureate, Dryden, would judge the best. Everyone scribbled silently and laboriously, except Dorset, who wrote down a few words quickly and flung the paper down on the table. After careful consideration, Dryden awarded first prize to the piece his lordship had written: "I promise to pay Mr. John Dryden or [*sic*] order five hundred pounds on demand."[7]

Upon the walls of the Poet's Parlor are inscribed the names of the outstanding writers of the Restoration: Edmund Waller, Matthew Prior, Thomas Flatman, John Dryden, William Congreve, William Wycherley, Thomas Otway, Thomas Hobbes, John Locke, Samuel Butler, Abraham Cowley, Nicholas Rowe, William Cartwright, Sir Kenelm Digby, Alexander Pope. And it was Pope who wrote the final tribute to his patron—an epitaph inscribed upon Dorset's tomb at Withyham: "Dorset, the grace of courts, the Muses' pride, Patron of arts, and judge of nature, died . . ."[8]

Knole in the eighteenth century was still a literary salon and a beneficent refuge for literati. Charles Sackville, second Duke of Dorset, seemed a bit eccentric; a proud, melancholy man, he produced operas and spent vast sums on singers. He wrote some verses, but he scarcely deserves to be called a poet. However, he lived only four years in his dukedom. The third Duke of Dorset was more interesting; for, a handsome man and gracious, he was beloved of all women. When this gay duke became ambassador in Paris, he patronized the ballet. There he fell head over heels in love with an Italian dancer, Giannetta Baccelli; he gave her his emblem of the Order of the Garter to wear as a hair-ribbon with the motto *"Honi soit qui mal y pense"* set in diamonds. When Giannetta returned to England with him, she was installed in one of the towers at Knole, which to this day remains known, through the mispronunciation of the English servants, as "Shelley's Tower." Dorset had Baccelli painted by Reynolds, drawn by Gainsborough, and sculpted in the nude. But eventually the Duke separated from his Italian dancer and married an heiress, Arabella Diana Cope, who bore him three children.

The history ends with the occupation of Knole by Victoria
Sackville-West's grandfather. She remembered him at Knole as
a taciturn, unsociable old man; yet, as we have seen in Chapter
I, these two—the child and her grandfather—were much alike
and understood each other. *Knole and the Sackvilles* is, on the
whole, interesting and readable, at least to the historian; Miss
Sackville-West peppers it with concrete details, anecdotes, and
lively descriptions. She communicates her own enthusiasm to
the reader.

III   Pepita

V. Sackville-West's strange grandfather was Lionel Sackville-
West, fifth son of the fifth Earl de la Warr; his lifelong attachment to his mistress, Pepita, the Spanish dancer and Victoria's
grandmother, is the subject of Miss Sackville-West's best-known
biography. *Pepita,* published in 1937, is, according to its author,
straight biography; everything in the book, she claimed, is true.
It furnishes indeed a fine example of the cliché that "truth is
stranger than fiction." Its color and lively tone make it most
interesting, and it is beautifully written. As a result of these
qualities, it deserves to rank among her finest achievements.

In 1852, Lionel Sackville-West was a young attaché to the
embassy at Stuttgart, when he met Pepita while on a Paris
vacation. The two fell violently in love, but Pepita had been
married to a Spanish dancer, Juan Oliva, years before, although
they were now separated. They had been married when both
of them were very young and when Pepita was an unknown
dancer. But, pushed by her determined mother and by her own
flair for the dramatic, Pepita won fame—not because she was
such a fine dancer but because she was a natural artist. However, although the whole world loved her—and a score of men
always worshiped at her feet—the quiet, young Englishman
carried off the prize. They never married—even though Lionel
tried; in fact, at one time his superior locked him in a hotel
room so that he would not ruin his diplomatic career by such
a marriage. Still, he remained loyal to her. Their first child, a
boy named Maximiliano León José, was born in 1858; four
years later the second child, Victoria Josefa Dolores Catalina,
arrived; and it was she who became V. Sackville-West's mother.

In all, Lionel and Pepita had five children (not counting one girl who lived only seven months); and Pepita died in childbirth when Victoria Josefa was only nine years old.

Book Two concerns not Pepita but her daughter, the mother of Victoria Sackville-West. At the death of Pepita, Lionel Sackville-West sent his daughter to a convent in Paris. When she entered, the young Victoria could neither read nor write. But she remained at the convent until she was eighteen when a Mrs. Michel Mulhall appeared to take the young girl to England. There she discovered an uncle, Lord de la Warr, who owned Buckhurst—and another uncle, Lord Sackville, who owned Knole. She also discovered two aunts: the Countess of Bedford and the Countess of Derby. Her father had just been appointed British Minister to Washington, and his eighteen-year-old daughter joined him there as his official hostess. We can imagine the furor and gossip caused by this pleasure-loving, beautiful girl in Washington society. Even President Arthur, then a widower, sought her hand.

Because of a diplomatic blunder, Lionel Sackville-West was recalled; but he soon found himself Lord Sackville, successor to his brother, and heir to Knole. At twenty-seven, Victoria was mistress of the estate—and in love with her first cousin, Lionel Sackville-West, five years her junior. They were married in the chapel at Knole on June 17, 1890. The young Lionel was seemingly as much in love with Knole as with his Spanish-beauty wife.

But now villainous treachery threatened to snatch Knole away. Pepita's son Henri, tired of farming in South Africa and now living in Paris, decided to claim both the peerage and the estate. He contrived to have the marriage entry of Pepita and Juan Oliva disappear (he wished to prove that they had never been married), and he declared that he was a legitimate son. The case was in the papers; Knole was closed; but eventually (as we saw in Chapter I) Sir Lionel won the lawsuit, and the family returned triumphantly to Knole. With perceptive objectivity Vita Sackville-West wrote, "to all of us Knole meant as much as any human being." But, she went on, "it [love of Knole] was different from one's love for any human being."[9]

Describing her mother and the parental environment, Miss Sackville-West declared their home a completely unintellectual one. Her mother, on one side, had the heritage of the opulent

English Sackvilles; but, on the other side, she had inherited
the Latin spirit of the Spaniards; consequently, she was a mix-
ture of conventionality and unconventionality. "No wonder I
loved," Vita wrote, and "wondered. No wonder my father loved
and got hurt."[10] Much as these two loved each other, they were
ludicrously ill-matched.

At the end of World War I, when her father had just returned
home after his army service, the three of them seemed to be
living contentedly together when the final storm broke. Sir
Lionel said mildly; "Oh look here, dear, would you mind telling
Sace—the bailiff—when you want any work done in the house?
Because, if you don't give warning, it upsets all the men's work-
sheets for the week on the estate." At this point, his wife lost
her temper, said that he had insulted her, burst into tears, and
left the room never to return. For the rest of their lives, Victoria
was torn between them; she saw each parent's side but she
was unable to effect a reconciliation between the two.[11]

This book is of great importance to an understanding of some
of the contradictions in Victoria Sackville-West's own nature.
Moreover, biographical details and actual events in the family
history furnished her with characters and situations for her
fiction.

IV Joan of Arc

Of Miss Sackville-West's notable biographies, three—*Joan of
Arc, The Eagle and the Dove,* and *Daughter of France*—form,
with *Pepita,* an eminent contribution to this literary genre. Before
writing *Saint Joan of Arc* (1936), V. Sackville-West asked herself
why another life of Joan was necessary. One of her answers is
that the Joan of Arc legend becomes a new symbol for each
generation; another is that the elements of mysticism in Joan's
religious life held great appeal for V. Sackville-West. But one
answer which the author does not give is her command and
understanding of the French and their language. It is obvious
that this work was prepared painstakingly and lovingly; literally
years of research went into the piece. It seems to me, however,
that V. Sackville-West, passionately involved with this character,
sought to find the "inner" Joan, the real Joan. But the problem
is—and perhaps always will be—that Joan remains an elusive,

un-real figure; the legends and the contradictions prevent finding her true character. Those who have written about her disclose generally more about themselves than about the Maid. Miss Sackville-West's Joan does come alive; but, as with George Bernard Shaw's creation, we feel that the Maid is more V. Sackville-West than an historical figure.

One of the best parts of the biography is that dealing with Joan's childhood and parentage. She was not a poor peasant's daughter; in fact, her family was distinctly bourgeois and was well thought of in the neighborhood. That Joan could neither read nor write was not an unusual situation at that time for young women of all classes, for there was no need for such education. The two dominating influences in her early life were also natural since they were potent forces in the climate of opinion: the church, and the war against England. Joan's deep piety and her enthusiasm for the glamor of soldiering were then natural. Patriotic feeling ran high, as it does in wartime; and Joan was a high-spirited, dedicated, idealistic young person.

Very graphic is the description of her escape from her family. On a visit to a cousin, she persuaded him to lend her boy's clothing and to help her secure a horse—then off she rode to Dunois. As to the question of why Joan dressed as a man, Miss Sackville-West, who herself preferred the easy freedom of slacks and boots, realized that masculine dress was an absolute necessity for Joan who was to live an active life on horseback on the battlefield and among men.

Joan's power of persuasion, or her ability to inspire confidence, is less easy to explain on grounds of practicality or expediency. Her strength, of course, according to Miss Sackville-West's interpretation, was the self-confidence—the conviction she exuded because she believed so firmly in her "voices." In this respect, we must remember that people in Joan's day more readily believed in the supernatural, in "miracles," than we. As long as she appeared successful, all went well; people were eager to believe in a deliverer sent by God to free France. Undoubtedly, too, she was unwittingly a convenient "tool" for Charles and his party—until he was safely installed in power.

Joan's downfall Miss Sackville-West attributes to two characteristics: "she strikes me all too often as a person of inspiration but of unequal judgment, as a person with an objective but no

reasoned policy; as a person galloping headlong down a narrow
road never lifting her eyes over the landscape beyond; as a person
whose very weapon was her strength, her very strength her weakness."[12] The second cause of Joan's downfall is a common human
weakness; in fact, it was noted and recorded first by Machiavelli,
who, however, states the idea somewhat differently. "Not the
least queerness of each individual human life," Miss Sackville-
West notes, "is its insistence upon adjusting itself throughout to
the key imposed upon it from the first."[13] Changes in the climate
of opinion, in environment, in the affairs of man demand an
ability to adjust, said Machiavelli, which, however, those in
power either do not have or cannot exercise. Joan's downfall
was also caused by the fact that she was no longer a necessity
to Charles; she was a political "victim" but could not realize this.

Whenever Miss Sackville-West encounters a knotty problem
and cannot find the answer, she asks questions—raises the issues—
and leaves them unanswered. In this way, she explores all possible interpretations, and her work becomes intellectually honest
but also provocative. To the biographer of Victoria Sackville-
West, one passage of interpretation makes the reading of this
book most rewarding. In discussing Joan's religious feelings and
convictions towards the "voices" of her saints, Miss Sackville-
West has stated her own beliefs:

It is with reluctance that I intrude my own convictions, but at a
given moment it surely becomes imperative for any biographer of
Saint Joan to make his own position clear, even at the expense of
some declaration of personal faith, if only in order to avoid any
suspicion of personal prejudice. The words in which I must clothe
that declaration are trite, I know, but the conviction behind them
is serious and sincere. I will state, therefore, briefly, that I am not,
myself, what is called a "religious" person in the orthodox sense
of the phrase, nor yet a member of any organized church. I do,
however, confronted with the ultimate enigma, believe, and believe
deeply, in some mysterious central organizing force which the natural
weakness and insufficiency of human nature find it necessary to
symbolize in a name, an amalgam of fear and comfort, which you
may call God or Gott or Dieu or Job or Allah or X, or even "a pure
mathematician," without any reason *necessarily* to identify that force
with your own human conceptions of a good and evil. It follows
logically that, holding this belief, I share with my fellow-mortals the
ancient superstition which no scientific explanation has yet been

able to account for: the belief in what we conveniently call the
supernatural. I believe in it so profoundly as to quarrel with the
expressions super-natural or extra-natural. For me there is only
one comprehensive, stupendous unity of which we apprehend but
the smallest segment. My readings into Joan of Arc have done
nothing but increase my belief in the existence of that unity, and
also the belief that certain persons are in touch with, or, shall we
say, receptive to the influences of, a unity for which we have no
adequate name, the greater whole of which our own imagination
embraces but a tiny part. Without pretending to explain how or
why these persons should be thus favored, I accept the fact, with
the logical corollary that Jeanne must be regarded as prominent
among them. . . . I have suggested that neither of the two possible
lines of approach—the scientific and the religious,—is alone sufficient
to resolve the mystery. The religious, of course, offers the quicker
way out of the difficulty: blind acceptance, to some minds, is more
agreeable than the more critical and enquiring attitude. It would
simplify the whole problem if we could just believe that God set
three of his saints to instruct Jeanne; if we could throw ourselves,
in short, into the frame of mind of the good, believing Christian.
Unfortunately for some of us, this attitude is impossible blindly to
adopt. I have been painfully torn myself. There are moments when
I am not at all sure that the religious line of approach may not, in
the end, prove right; when I am not at all sure that instinct may
not, as usual, be proved to have taken the short cut rejected by
reason. They may both arrive at the same point in the end, only
instinct may be found to have got there first. I am not in the
unfortunate position of anybody torn between an instinctive reliance
on instinct, and a reasonable reliance on reason.

In the meantime it seems to me that the only spirit in which to
approach the problem of Jeanne's voices and visions, in the present
state of our understanding, is a spirit of complete open-mindedness
and acknowledgment of our ignorance.[14]

Long though this quotation is, it states concisely and exactly
(in language not trite but simple), a profound and earnest
belief. It accounts for the philosophy of the novels: a conviction
in the power of love; acceptance of the mysterious, the incom-
prehensible; and faith in an omnipresent force that unifies and
pervades all things. It is interesting, in this connection, to recall
a letter in the second volume of *The Diaries and Letters of Sir
Harold Nicolson*, written during World War II by Vita to her
husband, in which she declares that she cannot understand his

disbelief in God; for her there simply must be a Supreme Spirit,
call it what we will.[15] In short, Vita was a "mystic" in a rational
sort of way.

IV The Eagle and the Dove

Miss Sackville-West's knowledge of French and of France
also stood her in good stead, during the writing of her next
biography, *The Eagle and the Dove: A Study in Contrasts*
(1943). And the "mystic" quality of her convictions is again
apparent, for this book presents the reader with the biographies
of two saints: St. Teresa of Ávila (1515-1582) and Ste. Thérèse
of Lisieux (1873-1897). These two Theresas were opposites: as
the title indicates, the Spaniard was more the eagle, the intellectual; the French woman was more the dove, the emotional.
The first was more masculine; the second, more feminine. Both
of them were "mystics."

The title of the book is derived from a poem of Richard
Crashaw's about St. Teresa:

> O thou undaunted daughter of desires!
> By all thy dower of lights and fires;
> By all the eagle in thee, all the dove;
> By thy large draughts of intellectual day;
> And by thy thirsts of love more large than they. . . .[16]

Teresa came of a fine, ancient, and well-to-do family. Her
father, Don Alonso, had been twice married: there were three
children from the first marriage and nine from the second; and
Teresa was born of the second union. Her mother was an invalid,
and from her Teresa acquired a taste for reading, especially
romantic tales; but Don Alonso had taught his daughter to read.
Still, she was also a sociable young woman—one much inclined
towards love and a voluble talker with a gay and humorous
disposition. As a young girl, she showed little but a frivolous
nature: she liked clothes and was vain about her appearance;
she flirted and engaged in the usual pastimes of youth.

Then a black three months came into her life. In her autobiography, Teresa referred only vaguely to this period; but she
accuses herself of a "mortal sin" which concerned an intimacy
with a girl cousin and another (apparently also a female), and

we note that in her own country Teresa's name is associated with Sappho's. Whatever her sin, Teresa was promptly put into a convent. At first, she had no intention of becoming a nun; in fact, the idea was repugnant to her. But after eighteen months she was considering it. In addition to her objection to marriage, there was another factor: fear. Afraid that, if she were to die, she would go to Hell, she saw the religious state as the safest.

When she began to have visions, she—a woman of breeding and culture, capable, and not unworldly—found these visitations embarrassing; and she tried to hide them from her companions. But the immediate effect was illness, which drove her to seek health at home and at her sister's country estate. She was so ill that she despaired of her life; and, when she had recovered sufficiently to inform her father of her decision to become a nun, he was displeased. So she ran away from home and entered the Carmelite Convent of the Encarnación. Again she became violently ill—and for three years she remained partially paralyzed. When she began literally to crawl around again, she was still only twenty-four. Of course, we cannot know the true nature of her illnesses, nor of their relationship to her visions. But she herself expressed a skeptical surprise and a distaste for the spectacular which seem sincere.

In the meantime, she was living both an active life and a contemplative life. She tried to find a few minutes to write, but her writing was constantly interrupted by her duties. Yet she wrote *The Way of Perfection* in a little cell with no table or chair; and *The Interior Castle*, a work of two hundred and sixty pages, she wrote in four weeks; but her autobiography is her best. St. Teresa, who was noted for her executive ability, founded a convent at Ávila, known as the San José. Dedicated to a system of reform, she traveled about, establishing new houses and reorganizing old ones. Teresa became famous; and, after years of struggle, her reform was recognized by Philip II, who had always been friendly. After her death, miracles became associated with her body which rested above the high altar of the church at Alba.

The nineteenth-century Ste. Thérèse had a very different childhood from that of the Spaniard. Born of middle-class parents (both of whom had wanted to live monastic lives but had been refused by the church), her father was a jeweler and a watchmaker at Alençon; her mother, a lacemaker. Mme. Martin had given birth to eight children when one evening, as she sat reading in the *Lives of the Saints,* she felt her shoulders clutched violently. This omen she interpreted as a sign of anger from the powers of darkness against the ninth child she was now carrying.

This baby, born on January 2, 1873, was christened Marie-Françoise Thérèse. Because little Thérèse was so small and delicate that her mother despaired of her life, the baby was sent to be nursed in the country in the cottage of Rose Taille, where Thérèse found health. But, when she was only four and a half years old, her mother died, leaving M. Martin in charge of five daughters. He decided to move to Lisieux, where he could have the help of his brother and sister-in-law in rearing his children. There the family was comfortable in a large house on the edge of town.

After her mother's death, little Thérèse became grave and religiously oriented. At nine, she sought to be admitted at the Carmel as a postulant; but the prioress told her that no postulants could be accepted until sixteen. When her sister Pauline took the veil, Thérèse became violently ill; and her life was despaired of. According to her own record, she prayed to the Virgin; and then she suddenly had a vision: the statue seemed to come to life, and Thérèse was cured.[17]

With her first communion, she felt the rapture of love, of a *fusion* with Jesus. Then occurred an incident which Thérèse called in her autobiography her "complete conversion"; it happened on Christmas Day, when she was nearly fourteen. As she was entering the house, thinking of her shoe filled with presents, she overheard her father say: "This is really too babyish a surprise for a big girl like Thérèse; I hope this will be the last year of it." These words, said Thérèse, pierced her heart; and she and her sister Celine had to stand for a few minutes to regain their composure. Then Thérèse ran downstairs, joyfully pulled out her shoe, and admired all her presents. Her father was pleased and laughed; but he had no idea of the victory over self that Thérèse had won. She had discovered her strength of soul.[18]

Before she was accepted at the Carmel, Thérèse went to Italy with her father. At an audience with Pope Leo XIII, she was one of the pilgrims who passed in single file, knelt, and received the Papal benediction. The guards had told the pilgrims that they must not speak, but Thérèse had other plans. As she kissed the

Pope's hand, she whispered, "Father, I have a great favor to ask of you. Allow me to enter Carmel at fifteen!" The Pope's reply was "Come now... you will enter if God wills it."[19]

Meanwhile, the Bishop of Bayeux had been busy negotiating with the Reverend Mother, and in April, 1888, Thérèse entered Carmel. The rules were strict, but not until near the end of her life did she ever complain of the hardships. Like Teresa of Ávila, she snatched moments to write poetry and her auto biography, *Histoire d'une Âme*. During Lent of 1897, she endured the fasting; but, on Good Friday, she had a bad hemorrhage of the mouth. Throughout the spring, she declined and yet welcomed death as the final union. After Thérèse's death the prioress had the autobiography printed; and it became enormously popular. Miracles began to be reported; and canonization finally took place in 1925.

Miss Sackville-West suggested that Teresa of Ávila was a "high-brow," born of the aristocracy and driven by an uncompromising intellect. Surely she was of the two saints, the more complex human being. Thérèse of Lisieux was the "low-brow" among Saints; born of the bourgeoisie, she possessed a simplicity and a naïve good nature. These two saints are remarkably drawn by Miss Sackville-West; if Teresa of Ávila seems more alive, perhaps it is because the author was more attracted by the stronger, intellectual figure. Certainly V. Sackville-West must have recognized a kindred spirit in this Teresa—both possessed a masculine intellectuality, a strong will, and a belief in mysticism.

But Miss Sackville-West was drawn to these two figures for several reasons. First of all, she was enough of a feminist to choose deliberately strong, significant women for study and portrayal. It is partly for this reason that the female characters in her novels are the best drawn. These two Theresas were interesting women who made contributions to the Catholic Church and to the society of their periods. Second, since both left autobiographies, the firsthand materials to give them life were available; moreover, the study in contrast that they afforded made an irresistible appeal to the literary artist. Third, and perhaps most important, this subject gave Miss Sackville-West an opportunity to explore certain aspects of mysticism which had always fascinated her. Teresa of Avila especially wrestled with the validity, the meaning, of the mystic experience, for V. Sackville-West believed that there were "mysteries" beyond the human understanding, at least for the present. But those of her friends who thought, after the publication of *Joan of Arc* and *The Eagle and the Dove*, that she would become a "candle-stick" did not thoroughly understand V. Sackville-West. Interested, even fascinated as she was by eternal mysteries, by "unexplainables," she was too much of a nonconformist, of a skeptic and an intellectual, to embrace the Catholic religion.

VI　Daughter of France

The fourth of the full-length biographies written by Miss Sackville-West is again from French history; for the *Daughter of France* (1959) records the life of Anne Marie Louise d'Orléans, Duchesse de Montpensier (1627-1693), who wrote her *Memoirs* with great frankness and a naïve ingenuity. And Miss Sackville-West made a penetrating observation when she wrote that, in writing autobiographies, the easiest of all forms of literature, the amateur may rival and sometimes surpass the professional. A degree of shapeliness is imposed by chronology; and, for the rest, a certain confusion matters not, may indeed give a greater impression of reality.

All her life the Duchesse was La Grande Mademoiselle—not at all pretty, she was very aggressive, and she was used to commanding people and to winning her own way at any cost. Much given to fads, Mademoiselle fancied herself a "blue-stocking": she wanted to learn Italian in order to read Tasso in the original. Then, like Marie-Antoinette, she adopted the rural life, dressed as a shepherdess, and gave elaborate picnics in the forest. Perhaps her chief attribute, which endeared her to Miss Sackville-West, was her love of houses. From her earliest years Mademoiselle enjoyed visiting estates small and large, a pastime she shared with her father. In her *Memoirs*, she never failed to comment upon these houses; sometimes she simply called them *"assez jolie,"* but she sometimes became poetical about them. When she arrived by torch-light at Valençay, she thought it a magical place. When she retired to St.-Fargeau, after being driven out of Paris, she hired François Le Vau, architect-brother of Louis Le Vau, who had designed Versailles, to remodel her house. When the work at St.-Fargeau was completed, Mademoiselle switched her affections to Eu and renovated it.[20]

Although Miss Sackville-West has communicated the vitality, the restlessness, and the volatile temperament of Mademoiselle, the portrait of her remains, at least for me, sketchily drawn. She does not emerge in depth; I do not feel that I understand her. However, the setting and the picture of French society in the seventeenth century are depicted with meticulous care. Indeed, the setting is so elaborate that it often crowds out the main character. And the necessity of including the complexities of the political history of the period increases the obfuscation.

VII   *V. Sackville-West, Literary Historian and Critic*

The final type of non-fiction written by V. Sackville-West is literary criticism, and we may only wish that she had written more of it because her perceptive penetration led her to reveal the essential quality of her subject's writing. For example, in her essay "George Eliot," Miss Sackville-West expressed the thesis that George Eliot was no rebel by temperament and that she tried to "fulfill her congruously unconventional destiny as conventionally and decently as possible."[21] Because of this essential quality in her personality, George Eliot quite sensibly realized that her best material lay in the familiar rural countryside and in the ordinary people met on the village street. But Sackville-West perceived the chief weakness of this writer's art; like most realists, George Eliot had a romantic side. She created heroes who are impossibly romantic scamps or prigs, and she wrote one badly sentimental novel, *Romola*.

Again, with an intuitive understanding, V. Sackville-West wrote a short biography of a female literary scamp—*Aphra Behn: The Incomparable Astrea* (1640-1689). In spite of her infamous reputation, Aphra Behn was a real "pro," the first Englishwoman to earn her living by her pen. Of all her novels *Aroonoko* alone is still readable in Miss Sackville-West's estimation. Like an early Mae West, Aphra Behn's essential quality was sex—her own life, most of her novels, and all of her plays deal with only one theme—sex.

In Andrew Marvell, Miss Sackville-West found a kindred spirit. Although Marvell's nature was not profound, it contained a genuine vein of poetic inspiration. While employed as a tutor at

Lord Fairfax's estate, he wrote his best poetry, including "To His Coy Mistress." This brief biography discloses Sackville-West's ability to make a cool, logical appraisal; for, when she discusses Marvell as a nature-poet, she points out his two main gifts: his presentation of the actual, precise detail; and his sense of man's harmony with nature. Next, she presents Marvell as a pastoral poet who united the pastoral tradition with the Cavalier-courtly style. As he matured, Marvell wrote poems in the Metaphysical vein, as a poet of the School of Wit. Finally, Marvell emerges as a satirist. But Marvell the nature-poet Miss Sackville-West found most congenial; and his preoccupation with the desire for a union of man with nature was one of Miss Sackville-West's own favorite ideas and the thesis for her novel *Grey Wethers*.

At a meeting of the British Academy of Arts and Sciences Miss Sackville-West read a paper on Walter de la Mare, which was later published in the *Proceedings*. To Miss Sackville-West, de la Mare was greatly misunderstood; indeed, he is generally remembered only as a poet of whimsical lyrics or of children's poetry. In this paper Miss Sackville-West examined an aspect of his attitude towards life, his *Weltanschauung*, which is best expressed in his poem "The Traveller." De la Mare is haunted by the fate of man, by the "riddle" of his experience on earth, and by the ultimate mystery of death. These matters are his permanent preoccupation, and "The Traveller" is his finest expression of these problems. In this poem, which is of course symbolic of Everyman's journey through life, a man on a white Arabian mare set out across a tract of country. He suffers from heat and cold, from thirst and hunger, from exhaustion; but worst of all, he suffers from dread and *fear*. This suffering is the ultimate reality. Miss Sackville-West's conclusion is that de la Mare pushed the frontiers of consciousness a step farther back for us "and, after all, is that not the supreme function of all art?"[22]

VIII *Conclusion*

The ability of Sackville-West to pierce through to the core of the artist and to perceive at once the essentials is well exemplified in her article about de la Mare; and this quality makes her a good biographer and critic. Her logical organization and her elegant yet simple style also make her non-fiction a delight to read. In her non-fiction, she seldom let her style gain the upper hand; consequently, these prieces are generally easy to read and are excellent examples of clear, straightforward writing. But what makes much of her non-fiction readable for us are the autobiographical bits, the personal "asides"; for they give us new insights into the personality of V. Sackville-West and thus aid us in understanding her other writings.

CHAPTER 4

Poet

"Even if you never wrote another line of
poetry, your fame as a poet is anchored in
The Land." —Sir Harold Nicolson[1]

IN *Pepita*, Victoria Sackville-West described Lady Sackville's
endeavors to promote her daughter's writing career. "I must
say," wrote Vita, "I writhed in embarrassment when I heard
of my wretched novels going to cabinet ministers, ambassadors
and the Queen. It was in vain. She thought it was a good way
to get better known and to make money. I said I didn't really
mind about getting better known and as for making money,
it was very nice if one could, but it came second,—a long way
second. I protested mildly that *The Edwardians* had sold quite
well, adding that I was sorry about that, because I hated writing
novels; was a bad novelist; would never be a good one; and
really only cared about writing poetry and other things."[2] But
to the present-day reader, Sackville-West's estimate of her own
writing ability comes as a surprise. Not only is she a competent
novelist, she is remembered primarily—at least in the United
States—for her contributions to the novel as a genre and for at
least two very fine novels—novels that will likely become part
of the permanent literature of the language: *All Passion Spent*
and *The Edwardians*. However, this quotation from *Pepita*
reveals the interesting fact that Sackville-West considered her
poetry better than her novels—or at least that she enjoyed writing
poetry more than writing novels; and it is true that she is
often at her best in the descriptive passages, in the turning of
the phrase, or in the establishment of a mood—all characteristics
which reveal the poet in her.

Although her poetry certainly deserves greater attention than
it is now receiving, the reason for its partial neglect is obvious.
Grant Overton has called her "A lady of the Tradition," meaning

58

that she wrote within the tradition, not away from it.[3] And poetry has advanced so rapidly in the *avant-garde* direction that Sackville-West's works may seem already "old-fashioned" in the Wordsworthian tradition. Another factor contributing to the "old-fashioned" quality of her poetry is the subject-matter; in love, as she always was, with nature, with gardens, and with gardening, and with the countryside, she very naturally wrote of these things. Most of her poetry is pastoral in theme: she followed the tradition of Theocritus, Virgil, and Edmund Spenser and the other Elizabethans. In spirit, she often seemed a belated Elizabethan; for the humanistic strain in Classical literature was strong in her. Also, her poetic forms are traditional. She wrote, as we shall see, in established meters and rhyme schemes.

I   The Land

One critic has said that V. Sackville-West had the courage to write an eclogue in the twentieth century—*The Land,* which won her the Hawthornden prize in 1927.[4] *The Land,* often described as a "gardener's manual in verse," is in reality more, much more: it expresses a way of life; a love of the countryside, of nature; and a profound sense of the oneness of kinship between earth and man. In all of these aspects her poetry resembles that of Wordsworth and the English Romanticists. This subject matter is surprising, I suppose, in an industrial era when poets sing no more of woods, or of the change of seasons, of apple-blossoms, or of a spring rain. Yet *The Land,* her finest poem, won her a widespread reputation in Britain as a poet. Harold Nicolson once wrote his wife, when she was despondent about her poetry, that "Your fame . . . is anchored in *The Land.* Scarcely a day passes that someone does not mention it."[5]

The Land is a long poem, mostly in blank verse, but with some rhyme. Its beginning is almost Virgilian in its pronouncement of subject:

> Hear first of the country that shall claim my theme,
> The Weald of Kent, once forest, and today
> Meadow and orchard, garden of fruits and hops,
> A green, wet country, on a bed of clay.[6]

Then follow four sections entitled "Winter," "Spring," "Summer," "Autumn." We can almost smell the fragrance of violets, the freshness of new-mown hay, the tang of hops drying in the oast houses. Yet country life is not sentimentalized; in fact, the austerity and hardships of the laborer's life are almost over-emphasized. The tone, on the whole, is quiet and somewhat dark. Symbolism has always been inherent in the eclogue form because the seasons correspond so naturally to the ages of man, but V. Sackville-West chose "Winter" to symbolize not death so much as re-birth, a waiting for the resurrection: "Since to live men labour, only knowing/ Life's little lantern between dark and dark."[7]

This quotation well illustrates V. Sackville-West's best poetic gift—a knack for the apt phrase which expresses economically and simply the idea. The reader is often surprised by such a phrase because its tone and color illumine the passage just as a highlight relieves the darkness of a painting; in fact, her poems often remind me of a Constable or a Turner painting. As here, her language and rhythms often sound Shakespearean. As she matured, her poetic diction became simpler, even laconic. She employed few figures of speech: her poetry at its best presents a universal idea—sometimes a rather ordinary one, or rather a basic one—in language that sings and creates a sharp image. We have, for example, the last line of the following:

> And August comes, when fields are sere and brown,
> When stubble takes the place of ruffling corn;
> When the sweet grass is like a prisoner shorn
> And summer makes a silence after spring.[8]

The idea of the ripeness of late summer, of a rest, after the dynamism of spring—its rushing growth, its vitality—is beautifully expressed in this last line. The passage well illustrates, too, the musical flow of her line—the rightness of the phrase not only to the idea but to the form. Although I have observed that she uses few figures of speech, in the following lines from *The Garden* we find a simile in which she achieves sharpness of imagery: "The yellow crocus through the grass will bring/ Her light as pointed as a candle flame."[9] Her musical ear taught her to break away from the monotony of the iambic pentameter rhythm. For example, in the section "Summer" of *The Land*,

she used octosyllabic couplets where the whimsical quality of
the subject matter calls for a livelier, brighter meter:

> In summer when the woods are deep,
> Ghostly society I keep,
> And play the spy, down dappled glades,
> On lovely or on ardent shades,
>
> . . . .
>
> And what's the matter, though I see
> A wrongly amorous company?
> Though lover after lover flit
> Labelled with names that do not fit?
> If Lovelace Saccharissa woo,
> Or Waller Julia pursue,
> If Marvell do Lucasta find
> Than his own Mistress less unkind,
> Or Herrick's persuasions prove
> A better argument of love,
> Than the conversion of the Jew?
>
> Perilla, fly! Corinna, stay!
> In deserts of Bohemia,
> A wood near Athens, or this wood
> Where these grown oaks as saplings stood,
> Three hundred years gone by,
> And yet I love her till I die.[10]

Her playful allusions to English pastoral poets, the "ghostly
society" which she keeps, are not only appropriate to the mood
and setting but also illustrate her strong sense of the long,
continuous, and eminent heritage of English poetry—a heritage
of which she was always aware and proud. And especially
strong in her was the Elizabethan strain of the heritage. She
felt an especial kinship with this period of English history.

For her, the past existed in the present and future; all three
met and merged in the instant. And, as she walked among the
oak trees in the Kentish Weald, it was natural for her to realize
that these trees were saplings when William Shakespeare wrote
of the "deserts of Bohemia," of "a wood near Athens," or of the
Oak Tree in Windsor Forest. And the "land"—this little isle—
was indeed what she loved until she died. The triteness of the
last line, taken from a famous seventeenth-century lyric, is

relieved by the twist in meaning, the "her" being, of course, England. In this passage the English literary tradition and the ancient heritage of English history are intertwined, as they always were in V. Sackville-West's mind and heart. Here are the seeds of the character Orlando: a point-of-view towards life that Virginia Woolf recognized in her friend, understood, loved, and satirized.

II The Garden *and Other Poems*

As a companion poem to *The Land*, Sackville-West wrote *The Garden*; but the composition of this second eclogue she found more difficult—perhaps because most of it was written during World War II and because the dignity of agriculture was lacking (gardens and seed-boxes are not so universal in appeal). Like *The Land*, this poem (published in 1946) won a prize—this time, the Heinemann Prize. In form, too, *The Garden* resembles the earlier poem: although blank verse dominates, it contains strophic stanzas and rhyme. Again Sackville-West uses the epic opening: "Small pleasures must correct great tragedies/ Therefore of gardens in the midst of war/ I boldly tell...."[11] Naturally enough, the poem is deeply tinged with the grief of war, with sorrow at the scars and wounds her dearly beloved English ground has suffered.

> Not only war, but natural Winter carries
> This valuable and enforced retreat,
> ....
> ....So the Winter gives
> A blameless idleness to active hands
> And liberates the vision of the Soul.[12]

This theme of the balm of solitude is, of course, a favorite one in Sackville-West's works, and the passage proceeds, in a Miltonic vein,

> Darkness is greater light, to those who see;
> Solitude greater company to those
> Who hear the immaterial voices; those
> Who dare to be alone.[13]

To her, solitude was a most essential need of life—as necessary as food and sleep.

Her poetry is deeply tinged with personal communings, with her inmost thoughts; therefore, it is through this medium that the reader often feels most closely drawn to the author. Not only did Sackville-West express her great need for solitude but her wonder at the essential mystery of life—another manifest conviction of hers:

> Should we resolve the puzzle, lose the zest,
> Should we once know our last our full intent,
> If all were staringly made manifest,
> The mystery and the elusive quest,
> Then less than ever should we be content.[14]

Her constant awareness of the mystery, which she called God, made every moment of her life intense and vital. Another basic idea is the ever-present hovering of death—the be-all and the end-all. Although it is natural that *The Garden* should be much concerned with death, composed as it was, during the blitz of London, at Sissinghurst, which was on the main line to London, we cannot help feeling that we have touched a vital spot in Miss Sackville-West's philosophy. We are reminded of *All Passion Spent,* which presents so poignantly the last days of a courageous woman. Even in "Spring" the presence of death is discovered:

> Though I must die, the only thing I know,
> My only certainty, so far ahead
> Or just around the corner as I go,
> Not knowing what the dangerous turn will bring,
> Only that some one day I must be dead,
> I still will sing with credence and with passion
> In a new fashion
> That I will believe in April while I live. . . .[15]

Again, it is the last line, with its sudden intensity that illuminates the whole passage.

"Summer" is filled with the horrors of war; and "Autumn" too is largely about death. The time is one of futility and despair, and we feel that this poem reflects the poet's mood:

> Yet Autumn calls for courage, as the end
> Of all things call for courage,—love or life:
> Seldom with clear-cut slicing of the knife,
> But a slow petering, a dismal droop.[16]

Sackville-West wrote poetry throughout her life. Her writing career began with the volume of verse—*Poems of East and West*; and, as late as 1944, she wrote, "If only I thought I could write good poetry I should not mind anything."[17] Her *Collected Poems* contains verses on a variety of subjects: on the death of her father, on ships, on Persia, on her love for England and for her husband. For me, one of her most successful poems is *Easter and Pentecost Enclose the Spring* (written in April, 1929), but for Harold Nicolson her best was *Sissinghurst* (1930), a long poem on the restoration of this medieval castle of her forebears. Together the Nicolsons had worked, on both the castle and the gardens, to make the estate one of the loveliest in England. To it Sackville-West had transferred her love of Knole; and Sissinghurst too had family roots for her, for Sir Thomas Sackville, the first Earl of Dorset, had married Cicely Baker of Sissinghurst. The following passage expresses not only the sense of ancient lineage but also her loss of Knole, scene of her childhood:

> A tired swimmer in the waves of time
> I throw my hands up: let the surface close;
> Sink down through centuries to another clime,
> And buried find the castle and the rose . . .
> Over my head the years and centuries sweep
> The years of childhood flown,
> The centuries unknown.
> I dream. I do not weep.[18]

Night, written for her husband, is a poem representative of her ideas and style. The following lines from the poem exemplify the lyrical flow of her verse and the simplicity of her imagery:

> Moonlight through lattice throws a checquered square:
> Night! and I wake in my low-ceilinged room
> To cherish silence deep with harmony;
> Sweet are the flutes of night-time, sweet the truce
> Lies between the day and day.
> . . . .
>
> My Saxon Weald! My cool and candid Weald!
> Dear God! The heart, the very heart of me
> That plays and strays, a truant in strange lands,
> Always returns and finds its inward peace,
> Its swing of truth, its measure of restraint,
> Here among meadows, orchards, lanes and shaws.[19]

This passage contains most of her favorite ideas, and evinces her Romanticism. The rhythm and cadence of her iambic pentameter in this stanza remind us of Wordsworth's. But her style is clean and precise; her diction, simple and direct. When we begin to fear that the feeling is about to spill over into sentimentality, she pulls in and whitens her style—as in the last two lines of the above quotation.

III *Conclusion*

In reply to a question from her husband about facility in finding rhymes, Sackville-West wrote that, as she grew older, she found no decreasing ability; on the contrary, she declared that rhymes came to her with such an "appalling virtuosity" that she felt like a juggler who could spin twenty plates at a time if he wanted to. However, her fear was that such facility might damage quality. Then, even more importantly, she wrote, "I feel I have immense control, and can say anything I like, however complicated and difficult. But I also feel that flatness has come with increasing competence."[20] But her fear was groundless; her long poems have plateaus, it is true; but what long poem does not? Then comes a peak: the reader encounters a sharp image, a lovely cadence, or an apt phrase, which at once picks up the intensity and re-establishes the poetic "quality."

Her husband also asked her whether she had difficulty in remembering when a line or phrase was by her or by someone else, and her reply is quite curious. She stated that she never could remember, and the first shock of this realization came when she had painstakingly hammered out a line, as she said, "choosing every word most carefully."[21] The line she finally arrived at was "Men are but children of a larger growth"—a line of Dryden's *Alexander's Feast*. (In one of the most interesting of the short stories in *Thirty Clocks Strike the Hours*, one entitled "The Poet," Sackville-West used the idea of a writer's subconscious at work, imitating and borrowing.)

Again concerning her musical sensitivity to rhythm and cadence, we have a description by Harold Nicolson of his wife's reading of her poetry at a very special occasion. In 1943, the Sitwells (Osbert and Edith) organized a poetry reading at Aeolian Hall for the benefit of the Free French. It was a royal party, for the Queen and the two princesses attended; and we find Miss Sackville-West among very distinguished company indeed—John Masefield, T. S. Eliot, Gordon Bottomsley, Arthur Waley, Edmund Blunden. Harold Nicolson tells us that he was moved by the presence of Poet-Laureate Masefield and much impressed by Eliot's reading of *The Waste Land.* During the intermission, the poets were greeted by the Queen. Then, during the second half of the program, Vita read *The Land.* "She stands there looking magnificent and modest and recites *The Land* quite perfectly. I hear a low murmur of delight passing through the audience. She was by far the best of the lot and I am so proud of her. She is as serene as a swan."[22] Even allowing for a husband's (and lover's) prejudice, Sackville-West's low voice and modest demeanor won her popular plaudits, just as they had on her American tour in 1933.

One more slim volume of verse that is interesting to read in connection with Sackville-West's own poetry was compiled by her and her husband during the war years, an anthology of their favorite poems—*Another World Than This* (1945); for much can be learned when we know what works of art from the past an artist admires. Husband and wife had long been in the habit of marking favorite passages and of writing notes or comments in the margins of the books they had read. (Young Dan Jarrold in *Family History* is delighted to discover that his friend and idol, Miles Vane-Merrick, marks his books because his own mother is forever chiding him for doing the same thing.) As the title indicates, this anthology presents an escape from the horrors of war and from the impending changes in the world which the authors knew and loved.

Again, as we would expect, the selections show a wide range of reading and understanding—a sense of continuity, of identity, with the past and a delight in sensuous beauty. The Nicolsons used a device of a calendar or almanac to present their selections: there are poems for each month of the year, selected and arranged according to four large categories—love, nature, philosophy, and miscellaneous. Poems from the Greeks to twentieth-century England are included; and, as we would expect, many came from the Renaissance. Most of the pieces speak of love, death, and nature; but death is ever-present in all seasons and in all months. With disasters of war all about them, the

Nicolsons' thoughts and feelings could hardly have been dis-
engaged from this subject.

In her concept of the function of poetry V. Sackville-West was
closer to the Renaissance poets, to the Romanticists (Wordsworth
and Keats), and to certain of the Edwardians (Yeats, Hardy,
Hopkins, de la Mare) than to the poets of the Bloomsbury
Group and the "avant-gardists" of the 1920's and 1930's. She
herself was aware of her lack of rapport with the modernists.[23]
Sackville-West is at her best describing the English countryside,
love, the emotions evoked by nature, and the seasonal cycles
related to the life of man. These subjects she expressed with a
dignity and a simplicity that we admire; and the musical quality of her diction, rhythm, and cadence delight the ear of any
sophisticated reader. It is rather too bad that her poetry is not
much read any more; there is much beauty to be found in the
best passages. True it is that she seldom expresses the anguish,
the despair, which she often felt; poetry was for her an escape
from life, from the tragedy of the world. But the poems are,
nonetheless, sincere and perceptive; they surmount the wasteland
and describe the well-wrought urn.

CHAPTER 5

Short-Story Writer

"Thirty Clocks Strike the Hours is a collection
of short stories of great distinction."
—E. L. Broun[1]

IT is a matter of regret that V. Sackville-West's short stories
are not better known. In many ways, they reveal her at her
best; and some deserve to rank with the finest in the English
language. Although there are only about a dozen of such merit,
all of them are finely cut gems, beautifully polished. The medium
is an especially happy one for Sackville-West because she is at
her best in painting a mood and in communicating an evanescent
emotion; and the short story is the perfect genre for this kind
of artistry. We lament the fact that she did not write more, for
there are only two volumes of her short stories.

I The Heir and Other Stories

The Heir and Other Stories (1922), which presents us with her
early work, contains tales on various themes; but all are written
with elegance and precision. The title story, "The Heir," has been
called the "perfect" love story.[2] Although this remark was made
somewhat humorously, it is at least a "perfect" short-story; for
its author, like the hero of the story, had, as we have seen, a
love-affair with at least two old mansions—Knole and Sissinghurst. In "The Heir," Miss Phillida Chase, owner of Blackboys,
a fine old English estate, has died, leaving the place to her
nephew, Peregrine Chase. Mr. Chase, a bachelor and an ac-
countant, has lived a dull, middle-class sort of existence before
he inherited Blackboys. When he goes to the estate, he is told
by his aunt's lawyers that his inheritance is badly entailed and in
debt; therefore, he should sell the property to a real-estate de-
veloper, auction off the manor-house to a wealthy American,

68

and dispose of the furnishings. He also meets his aunt's butler, a fine old retainer who loves the house, and a friend of his aunt, Colonel Stanforth, who also hates to see the old place go.

Mr. Chase realizes that he ought to sell, but, gradually and subconsciously, the tranquility of the country and the deep sense of tradition grow upon him. Although he does not realize what is happening, he knows that, as the time for the auction approaches, he grows restless and uneasy. On the day of the auction, he appears; and in desperation, as he realizes how much the old house has come to mean to him, he bids wildly to retain his possession. Mr. Chase, who was just an ordinary, timid Philistine *before* his inheritance, has been molded by the house and finally knows himself. The ending is superb; for, as he stands surveying proudly his new possession, the auctioneers and bidders having departed in high dudgeon, the butler asks whether the master will dine in the dining-room or on the terrace. The old house has won.

This short story is one of Miss Sackville-West's finest. Not only is the central idea, the power of the English tradition of noblesse oblige, presented in an original way but the story is also an almost perfect example of craftsmanship. The spotlight is consistently fixed upon Chase, the heir—and the other characters remain shadowy. The action proceeds straightforwardly, always developing the main character, whose metamorphosis is, however, implied and never forced. The style likewise is simple and direct, and the laconic ending is a superb touch. Moreover, the mood of the English countryside is delicately evoked.

The next story in the collection, "The Christmas Story," is a macabre tale—one which we do not find pleasant but one which we never forget. When the story begins, Lydia Protheroe (née Alice Jennings) is a successful costumier and wigmaker. Forty years ago she had inherited a little money when she had come of age and thereupon had announced to her family that she was leaving home to open a shop dealing in theatrical costumes and wigs. Her bourgeois family was aghast: her parents, her brother, and her sister denounced her; her father turned her out. No one in the family was to disgrace them all by associating with theater folk. So Alice Jennings left home, assumed the name of Lydia Protheroe, opened her shop, and became famous as a theatrical costumier and wigmaker. She worked hard, lived above her shop, had nothing to do with anyone, and heard nothing from her family.

When Bertie, her brother, writes to disclose that, after all, they should become friends and forget the past, Lydia replies by inviting the family for Christmas. Then she proceeds to lay her plans: her family once had disowned her; now that she is wealthy and successful, they want to come; she will pay them back. Indeed, she has waited for forty years for the opportunity. On Christmas Eve, Bertie and his wife, as well as Emily and her husband, arrive. The place is eerie, and Lydia is strange. After she locks her guests in their rooms, they hear strange noises at night. At breakfast on Christmas morning, they find presents at their places: a red nose for Bertie, a blue wig for Bertie's wife, a pair of ears for Fred, a black moustache for Emily. Lydia insists that her guests wear these grotesqueries; when they protest, she produces a gun. At Christmas dinner, she plies them all with wine—and gloats over the drunken caricatures lolling at the table. The story ends as carolers from the village enter, and Lydia sardonically introduces her neighbors to her family.

The mood and setting of "The Christmas Party" are vividly communicated: the eerie, ghostly atmosphere in the house; the grotesque, fantasylike quality of the family gathering. Sackville-West very cleverly uses the masks as symbols of the bourgeois affectations and false fronts of the members of Lydia's family. And Lydia, once a young rebel against society, herself becomes a grotesquerie through a long-consuming hate.

We cannot pause to examine the rest of the short stories in this collection, but they are all worth-while and beautifully designed ones. They reveal not only a rich versatility in theme but also a perceptive, intuitive understanding of people's inner lives. Almost all of them have a bit of fantasy, of the supernatural; and many are marked by a touch of the macabre.

II   Thirty Clocks Strike The Hour

Seven years later an even finer collection of short stories was published—*Thirty Clocks Strike the Hour* (1929). The qualities noted in the first collection (her gift for creating a mood, a touch of fantasy, and her ability to probe into the inner life of a character) are present in these stories, but, in addition there are, as we shall see, a deftness and sureness of touch that betoken

Sackville-West's complete technical mastery of her medium. The title story, which may have come from the author's own experience, is told in the first person by a young girl who is visiting her great-grandmother in Paris; and its mood reminds us of that in *All Passion Spent*. The speaker hides behind a tapestry to watch the very old lady, fragile and feeble, come into the ballroom, which is now dusty and tarnished but still elegant, to hear her thirty clocks chime; for one duty of her butler is to set and wind the clocks for this daily ritual. Feebly, hobbling on a cane, the little old lady walks by the clocks; but, as she hears the chimes she comes to life, straightens up, and a spark gleams in her eyes. Then, when the chimes have ceased, she becomes once again the fragile old lady; the spirit flickers and dies. This little piece is really a gem; it is a *vignette* done in pastels. The spirit of a former age is so vividly expressed that we see the tarnished ballroom with its two old people moving like figurines doing a minuet, and we smell the fragrant mustiness of the Edwardian period. Perhaps the key to the success of this short story is its "specificness"—the virtue of its descriptive details.

The next story, "The Death of Noble Godavary," is a variation upon a favorite theme of Miss Sackville-West's: the clash of the Latin and English temperaments, a subject she knew firsthand; for the Spanish strain that she had inherited from her grandmother Pepita, one still strong in her mother, was also evident in Sackville-West's personality. On an estate in the North of England lived Noble Godavary, with his Italian wife and her daughter Paola. Upon the death of Noble, it is discovered that Paola has inherited the estate. The English relatives are dismayed, for it has been apparent that neither the Italian wife nor her daughter has any love for this drab and gloomy land. So Paola destroys this life that she so hates by opening the sluice of the dam. She is now free—free to return to Italy. Except for its descriptions of this gloomy Northern section of England, I find this story less satisfying because the main characters are not convincing; they seem to have no depth.

In "Gottfried Kunstler," the next story, Gottfried falls and hits his head one Sunday in December, 1523, when everyone in the village is ice-skating; and thereafter he suffers from amnesia. A spinster, Anna Rothe, takes him to her home; and the two of them live together in seclusion—and in perfect happiness. They become different people; their personalities flower. They skate together, roam the woods together, sit in her little cottage together. The winter passes, and then one day Gottfried's wife comes. Upon recognizing her, Gottfried changes, becomes his old self, and seems to recall nothing of his life with Anna; and the townspeople, claiming that Anna transformed Gottfried, burn her as a witch. The beauty of this short story lies in the account of the innocence of the love affair, in the power of love to bring fulfillment of the personality. The intricacy of the relationship between Anna and Gottfried is delicately handled.

"The Poet," which presents another interesting theme, about artistic creation, is told in the first person by a man vacationing in Italy; he meets the poet at a café; they talk and become friends. The poet, obviously poor and ill, lives only for his poetry; and he is convinced that he will be recognized as England's greatest poet, except, possibly, for Shakespeare. When the poet dies, the teller of the tale goes to the poet's room; for he has been appointed executor. The only legacy is, of course, the poems. They are without doubt good, but all of them are the known works of other poets. One only, except for the opening line, seemed original:

> When I am gone, say only this of me:
> He scorned the laurels and the praise of men,
> Alien to fortune and to fame; but then
> Add this: he plunged with Thetis, in the sea;
> Lay naked with Diana in the shade;
> He knew what paths the wandering planets drew;
> He heard the music of the winds; he knew
> What songs the sirens sang; Arion played.
> Say this; no more; but when the shadows lengthen
> Across the greensward of your cloistered turf,
> Remember one who felt his sinews strengthen
> And tuned his hearing by the line of surf.
> One who, too proud, passed ease and comfort by,
> But learned from Rome and Hesiod how to die.[3]

This sonnet, which seems to embody the thoughts of all poets, is perhaps a masterpiece of pastiche! We remember that, when Harold Nicolson once asked his wife if she had difficulty in knowing whether a phrase or line was her own or another's, she replied that she never could. "The Poet" is one of Miss

Sackville-West's new ventures into irony, a device she handled especially well in one novel, *Seducers in Ecuador*. The poet, who has spent his lifetime glorifying the poetry of the great, thinks to attain thereby immortality for himself.

Among the other short stories in the book is "Panodoro," the name of a little Italian fishing village where an Englishman, a romantic intellectual, has found peace. When he falls in love with village-beauty Amata, he imagines what an idyllic life he could enjoy here with her as his wife. One day, however, he is shocked out of his dream world by the return to his native village of Tito, Amata's fiancé, who is going to take her with him to New York—and the two young Italians cannot wait to leave their dull, sleepy Italian village for the vulgar delights of New York City, which Tito has so glowingly pictured. The dramatic irony of the situation is charming—and surprising.

Another short story, "Elizabeth Higginbottom," is a vignette of a forty-year-old spinster who yearns for romance and love. She falls for the office Romeo, Sylvester Scroggs. In a moment of boredom and pique at being discarded by his girl friend, he promises Elizabeth to take her to the theater. After Elizabeth invites him to come to dinner at her apartment, she lives in anticipation of this evening. And, of course, Sylvester Scroggs breaks the date when he had a chance to go out with his girl friend. This story well exemplifies Miss Sackville-West's ability to get inside a female character and portray her inner emotions and daydreams. It also shows the influence of the stream-of-consciousness school.

"Up Jenkins" is a sensitive story about four young people—Michael, Simon, Judith, and Anne—who pride themselves on their emancipation: their freedom from the shackles of love affairs and from the inhibitions of bourgeois society. While they are vacationing together, both men fall in love with Judith. When Simon and Judith finally wander off on the beach at night, Michael and Anne go after them—but, seeing the couple caught up in their love, Anne puts out her hand to Michael, saying "Come away. It's real, don't you see—it's real."[4] Again the all-consuming, over-powering force of love is Sackville-West's theme; but it is perceptively expressed through the emotions of these four young people.

The final short story in the book "The Unborn Visitant" is

another gem that presents the problem of the difficulty of
one generation's understanding another; to do so, it depicts the
conversation between a mother and a daughter of the Edwardian
era. In 1908, a rather ordinary young woman, Elsa Branksome,
attracts the attention of the catch of the season, Evan Sinclair.
At a houseparty, he proposes; and she promises to give him her
answer in the morning. That night she discovers in her bedroom
a young girl named Daphne, who is the unborn daughter of
Elsa and Evan Sinclair. At first, Elsa is shocked by this young
lady and her talk of life in the 1930's; and she does not much
like her. But when, after urging her mother to hurry up and
marry Evan, Daphne disappears, her mother finds that she
has decided to accept Sinclair's offer of marriage. This story is
another instance of Miss Sackville-West's fascination in the
occult and in fantasy.

III   *Conclusion*

All of these stories are beautifully constructed and polished.
We are delighted by their economy, for not a word is wasted
and much is implied. Also, we participate in the experience;
like E. M. Forster, Miss Sackville-West demands that we bring
with us a rich understanding and a sense of awareness. Many of
these short stories deserve to rank among the finest in the language because they possess two essential qualities: the establishment of just the right mood and the successful communication
of subtle and delicate emotions of the characters. "The Heir,"
"Thirty Clocks Strike the Hour," "Gottfried Kunstler," and "The
Unborn Visitant" deserve inclusion in any anthology of English
short stories.

CHAPTER 6

The "Country" Novels

"I have a great love for the country people:
they are to me like the oaks of the land."
—V. Sackville-West[1]

V. Sackville-West's early novels are generally concerned
with England—the English countryside and the English
folk. Her intense love and concern for those subjects associate
her with E. M. Forster, one of the Bloomsbury Group whom
Miss Sackville-West especially admired. But, unlike Forster and
like Thomas Hardy, she generally localized her countryside—
the Dorset country and the Weald of Kent. And, as in Hardy's
novels, the countryside or setting sometimes becomes an actual
character in the novel; nature helps to mold the characters and
to advance the plot. Furthermore, Sackville-West had a mystic,
almost pantheistic feeling for nature that suggests Wordsworth
and Coleridge but which is also very much in the mainstream
of nineteenth-century English literary tradition.

I Heritage

Heritage, which appeared in 1919 when the author was twenty-
seven, is Miss Sackville-West's first published novel. The book
opens in the Italian village of Sampiero della Vigna Vecchia,
where the "I," the speaker in the story, meets Christopher
Malory—an independent, rather eccentric intellectual and ro-
manticist. On the narrator's last day at Sampiero, Malory relates
the story of his past, a series of experiences that took place in
Kent, England. Malory had decided to try farming; for in
his own words,

I have a great love for the country people; they are to me like the
oaks of the land, enduring and indigenous, beautiful with the beauty
of strong, deep-rooted things, without intention of change. I love

in them the store of country knowledge which they distil as resin
from the pine, in natural order, with the revolving seasons. I love
the unconsciousness of them, as they move unheeding, bent only
on the practical business of their craft. I revere the simplicity of
their traditional ideals. Above all, I envy them the balance and the
stability of their lives.[2]

The irony of this last statement is borne out by the events that
follow, when Malory goes to work at Amos Pennistan's farm.
Besides Mr. and Mrs. Pennistan, the household consists of the
old great-grandmother, three sons, and two daughters, Nancy
and Ruth. The two daughters are very different: Nancy is a normal, simple country girl; but Ruth is a beauty and an enigma. Malory soon learns that the old grandmother was a Spanish dancer,
whom Oliver Pennistan (Amos' grandfather) had discovered and
had married. Born of this union were two children: one was
Amos' father, the other was Rawdon Westmacott's mother.
The Westmacott farm is next door to the Pennistan's; and its
present owner and sole inhabitant is Rawdon Westmacott, first
cousin of Amos Pennistan.

Rawdon Westmacott is twelve years older than Ruth, but they
have played together since childhood, and a strange attraction
between them exists. Their natures are much alike: both have
inherited the Spanish strain; both have passionate natures; a
stubborn willfulness; and a sense of the mysterious fatality of
life. Rawdon passionately desires Ruth; she is irresistibly drawn
to him but intuitively senses danger in their relationship.

During Malory's stay with the Pennistans, Nancy marries a
nice, ordinary farmer; Ruth, however, is reluctant to give herself
to Rawdon. It is obvious to the reader that she is in love with
Malory and admires his sophistication, but he is not aware of
Ruth's feeling; in fact, he urges her to break with her cousin
and to marry a good country lad (as her sister did)—one Leslie
Dymock. Realizing that Malory does not love her, Ruth at
length consents to marry Leslie; but, on the eve of her wedding, she runs away with Rawdon. This turn of events puzzles
Malory; he does not understand the feminine mystique.

Shortly after this event, Malory leaves the Pennistans; at this
point, his narration ends, for he and the speaker part company
and return to England. World War I breaks out, and both men
are engaged in the war. The "I" is wounded and discharged

from the army. Uncertain of his future and seeking the tranquility of the country, he goes to the Pennistans and calls upon Ruth at the Westmacott farm, where she is living with three children; her husband is in service. Their married life has been stormy. Rawdon, drunk most of the time, has mistreated his wife and has been unfaithful to her. The irony of fate intervenes: Nancy's husband is killed, but Rawdon returns. When domestic life grows worse, Ruth goes home with her children to her parents. Rawdon, in a black humor, pursues her. The speaker, who cannot stand the cruelty, goes to his room, brings down a pistol, and suggests that he stay with Ruth during the scene between husband and wife. Ruth persuades him to leave her alone with Rawdon, but she keeps the pistol. Outside, the speaker hears a shot; he runs into the kitchen, discovers that, when Ruth attempted to shoot (or at least to threaten) her husband, the gun had kicked back. Both Ruth and the speaker are defeated; Rawdon forces his wife and children to return.

The speaker now leaves—and the third and final section of the story begins. It is ten years later. The speaker receives a long letter from Malory. When the war had ended, he had wandered about, finally working with an archeologist for ten years at Ephesus, but always dreaming of Ruth. When Macpherson, the archeologist, had died, Malory had returned to London. While at his club, he is surprised by a visit from Ruth. She comes to ask his help, for her husband has finally left her and is in America. She tells Malory how Rawdon gradually disintegrated. His drinking and whoring grew worse; at times, he bullied Ruth, but most of the time he cringed from her, whined and pleaded. Now their roles were reversed; she ordered him about—and he obeyed her surlily, getting out of the house on any pretext.

One day, when she had stormed at him, letting loose all her pent-up resentment, he had replied: "There, it's over, he wailed, don't be afraid, Ruth, I won't touch you. Only let me go away now; it's this life has done for me. I can't live with you. You can keep the children, you can keep the farm; I'm going away, right away, where you'll never hear of me again. Only let me go."[3] When her story is finished, Malory realizes that Ruth has loved him from the first and that now they are free, free to be together. Life has begun for both of them.

The title, apparently, is intended to give us the clue to the

problem: the Spanish or Latin heritage. "What a train of dyna-
mite, isn't it, laid in the arena of Cádiz? What a heritage to
transmit even to the third generation!"[4] We remember, of course,
that Miss Sackville-West's own grandmother was Pepita. This
conflict between the English and Latin temperaments V. Sackville-West had observed firsthand and had pondered.

Katherine Mansfield believed *The Heritage* a failure because
there is no crisis. It abounds in "points of significance, but there
is no central point. After an excellent first chapter ... we begin
almost immediately to feel that the author, in dividing her story
as she does between two tellers, has let it escape from her control. ... The story falls into three pieces. We never know what
fear filled Ruth's husband. What Ruth did to provoke fear we
do not know."[5] Much of this criticism is true: there is no crisis,
the story does suffer by being told by two people, it does fall
into three parts, and the method of narrative is unduly complicated. The "I" begins the story; then Malory relates the action
of the past, but leaves the plot unfinished; the speaker and
Malory part company, and war keeps them apart; the "I,"
wounded and discharged, becomes involved with the characters
in Malory's past but leaves them again with the plot unfinished;
finally, ten years later, a letter from Malory relates the final
action and so the story ends. And, as to the crisis, I must agree
with Miss Mansfield that there is none: the structure of the novel
is not tight enough. However, I do believe that there is a central point: it is surely the inexplicability and inevitability of fate
(whether it is caused by environment or by heritage) as these
are shown in the lives of the two main characters, Ruth and
Rawdon. Although man's struggle against an indifferent fate
is in vain, it is nonetheless not without dignity.

And I think that we do know why Malory left Ruth, even
though the reason is not explicitly stated. The stoicism, the utter
contempt, the cold hatred in Ruth—coupled with Rawdon's own
sense of guilt and inadequacy—wear upon him and finally
destroy him. Just as Tess's innocence undermined D'Urberville
in Hardy's *Tess of the D'Urbervilles*, so does Ruth's integrity
and strength undermine Rawdon. We are reminded that the
power of the subconscious was another tenet of the Bloomsbury
Group. *The Heritage* is a psychological novel; the characters
are all important—their individuality, their motivations, their

interactions of personality, and their changes in character as influenced by the sequence of events.

Miss Mansfield proceeds to quote a passage from *Heritage* which she attributes to the author, but it is actually spoken by "I," the speaker, in the narrative. Like the "I" in Somerset Maugham's novels, Sackville-West's pretends not to understand the characters and their motives; and the quotation cannot, therefore, be identified with the author herself, nor is it fair to isolate it from its context. The passage does, however, contain Sackville-West's statement of purpose: it summarizes all the points I have been making—her concept of fate, her belief that what a person is is more important than what he does, and her faith in mystic forces in the universe, which are beyond human understanding.

Our [the speaker's] and Malory's error, I suppose, arose from our delusion that in this affair, which we considered peculiarly our own, we held in some measure the levers of control. Our conceit, as I see it now, was absurd. We were dealing with a force capricious, incalculable, surprising, a force that lurked at the roots of nature, baffling alike to the onlooker and the subject whose vagaries it prompted.

I should like to explain here that those who look for facts and events as the central points of significance in a tale, will be disappointed. On the other hand, I may fall upon an audience which, like myself, contend that the vitality of human beings is to be judged less by their achievement than by their endeavour, by the force of their emotion rather than by their success. . . . My difficulty throughout has been that I laboured with stones too heavy for my strength, and tried to pierce through veils too opaque for my feeble eyes. Little of any moment occurs in my story, yet behind it all I am aware of tremendous forces at work, which none have rightly understood, neither the actors nor the onlookers.[6]

The characters in her story have been formed by forces of heritage—the Spanish blood in Ruth's and in Rawdon's veins— and the significant actions in their lives are caused by the elemental power of the *id* within them. Their passionate temperaments clash with their environment. These forces, then, comprise fate, in Miss Sackville-West's terms—a concept of fate that differs from Hardy's which is rather one of environment and which is more naturalistic.

These early novels have another concept in common; they struggle with the "heart of darkness" theme—the origin of evil in the sons of Cain. Rawdon's problem, one that lies at the core of his personality, is exactly this: whence comes the darkness, the blackness within? The reason Ruth finally gains ascendency and Rawdon disintegrates is that the evil and guilt in Rawdon stem from fear, from cowardice towards life and fate. Ruth succeeds in overcoming her tragedy because she is strong and capable of loving; Rawdon is defeated because he is consumed by fear and hate.

II   The Dragon in Shallow Waters

In *The Dragon in Shallow Waters* (1921), Silas Dene exemplifies the same idea. He tries to flaunt fate, tries to manipulate events and people, and plays God; but when he is forced by two women in the story to face the truth—that he is at heart a coward —he too disintegrates. The title of this novel Miss Sackville-West has taken from a Chinese proverb: "The dragon in shallow waters *became* the butt of shrimps." The applicability of the title soon becomes apparent; Silas considers himself the dragon, but he is defeated by humble people, the shrimps.

The setting is not Kent but the Fen country; Lincoln is the nearest large town. The action takes place in a small village dominated at one end by a soap factory and at the other by the ruins of an abbey. The setting is a dark, grim one—the dour, cheerless countryside of the Brontës—suitable to the mood of the story and to the personalities of the characters. Among the workers in the factory are two brothers: Gregory Dene, who is deaf and dumb; Silas Dene, who is blind. The Dene brothers are shunned by the villagers, because they consider these two as "queer" and, therefore, as evil.

When the story begins, Gregory with his wife Nan lives in one-half of a cottage; Silas with his wife Hannah in the other side. However, word has just come to the Denes that Hannah's body has been found on the railroad tracks; she has been hit by a train. Nan, Gregory's wife, is the only one who mourns her death; for the two brothers seem impervious to any emotion. On the evening of the death, Nan goes to her side of the cottage to tidy up, leaving the two brothers alone. When she returns, she overhears Silas exulting in the success of his plan; he shouts to Gregory (who, although a deaf mute, seems intuitively to understand Silas) that he murdered his wife because she was faithless to him with Dounithorne, one of the factory hands. Whether she really was or not, we never know, but suspect not. Nan, of course, keeps her knowledge of Silas' crime to herself.

The squire of the neighborhood, who is also a director of the factory, is Malleson. His wife, Christine, hates her husband, is bored with country life, and is seeking a new diversion. She finds it in Silas. Hearing about his gift for oratory, his self-acquired knowledge, and his "queer mysterious ways," she sends for him. She wants to find out whether he actually can control his life—if he lives in absolute consciousness of the moment and if he is aware of this quality. Their meetings are a matching of wits; she tries to break his arrogance, to make him lose his self-control; he, on his part, is flattered by having an audience and is attracted to her. And Christine is attracted by the sheer physical power of this man, by his immense vitality.

In the meantime, Linnet Morgan, a young chemist employed at the factory, comes to live with Silas. He is in his twenties, about Nan's age—the Dene brothers are in their fifties. Naturally, the young people are attracted to each other; but they are innocent, unaware of their emotions, until Silas, pretending to be on their side, perceives their love and reveals it to them. He pretends to approve Nan's love for Linnet. At first, Nan is suspicious; but Linnet allays her fears, saying that they should pity Silas, the blind man, who has never known love. In his naïveté, Linnet has no understanding of Silas' true nature.

At about this time, Silas' son Martin returns home (Silas and Hannah had two children, a son and a daughter. Both of them, unable to endure the cruelty of their father, had left home.) When Martin learns from Nan of his mother's death, he at once accuses his father of causing her to commit suicide. Silas drives his son away again, and that night, as Silas lies in bed, we see his weakness: he cannot love. To him, "love's wholly a question of weakness, the weaker you are, the more desperately you love."[7]

Oftentimes Silas goes to the Abbey, to which he is drawn by a strange fascination; but he goes to pit his will against God's,

for Silas is the anti-Christ. After such occasions Silas is driven
to commit some crime. One time there is a fire, and Silas is
blamed for it by the villagers. Silas' reputation is becoming so
bad that Lady Malleson, realizing that her game is dangerous,
calls Silas to her to tell him that she is through with him and
that he is nothing but a coward, despite his fine philosophic
talk. This allegation Silas recognizes as the truth—and he is
beside himself with rage; now his revenge on a society he hates
becomes his only motive for living.

Silas' brother, Gregory, has suspected, all this while, nothing
of his wife's love for Linnet. Gregory, who is interested only in
his designs for machinery, spends every spare moment at his
drawings, redesigning the whole factory. When Mr. Calthorpe,
the overseer, discovers Gregory's aptitude and takes him to
Birmingham on a business trip, Silas has his opportunity to
make trouble. He spies upon the lovers, who, however, do
nothing wrong. Nan has made up her mind not to touch Linnet
while her husband is away and to tell him as soon as he returns
of her love for Linnet. The decorous behavior of the two young
people enrages Silas; he manufactures lies and writes to his
brother of his wife's infidelity.

When Gregory returns home, he is ready to murder Nan and
Linnet; and Silas is exultant at the success of his plan. He manages to persuade his brother to go to the factory, which is closed
for the evening, and he promises to send Linnet there after
him. Gregory can then kill Linnet—and Nan will be forced to
spend the rest of her life in misery, a slave to the Dene brothers.
But Nan, sensing trouble, goes to Silas to find out where Gregory and Linnet are. Silas will not tell her; he only enjoys her
agony and shouts, "the world's been black for me; I'll make it
black for others."[8] In desperation, Nan cries out that he is a
coward—"We all know you for a coward. We all know your
talk for bluster. Did you think we didn't know that, by now?"[9]
Once more Silas is forced to look inward—and to admit the truth.
Like Lady Malleson, Nan has laid bare his weakness and revealed the rot within him; and the inner walls of his defenses
crumble.

Robbed of his triumph, he runs to the factory, and Nan secretly
follows him. In the vat room, where the liquid soap is boiling,
Gregory has just knocked Linnet unconscious. Nan runs to res-

cue Linnet, while Silas turns to Gregory. Strangely, Gregory seems to understand Silas' change of attitude; and, like an animal, Gregory leaps to destroy Silas. But Silas is the quicker; he throws Gregory into a vat of the boiling yellow fat.

Trying to escape, Silas now runs out of the factory to the Fens. He has lost his reason; like a madman, he stalks the moors until he is hunted down. "He was full of a crazy, hopeless defiance." When captured, he screams, "What match is a blind man for clear-seeing men? You had me at a disadvantage all my life—all of you! You were orderly, while I struggled. Gone under! but not as tamely as you think."[10]

This novel is successful in creating moods and emotions: terror, malevolence, pity, fear, anger—all the "dark" aspects of man are presented. And the natural setting adds to the grimness: the Fens, the ugliness of the soap factory, the massive ruins of the Abbey. Man's potential for evil, the innate evil and cruelty, and the subconscious depths of the personality are the concerns of this novel. Miss Sackville-West possessed the ability to paint, with poetic precision, a mood or feeling—and to communicate the emotion to the reader. In these respects, the novel is brilliant. But the characters remain enigmas; they are phantoms that never emerge into the strong sunlight.

Three reasons for this weakness of the novel are obvious. First, the characters become vehicles for ideas, for attitudes towards life, which they seem to symbolize; they resemble puppets or figures in a morality play. Second, we are not taken inside the characters; we are told that they think this or feel that, but we do not participate in their inner life. Third, the characters are overdrawn; they are black or white, as in a melodrama. One consequence of this exaggeration is that they seem incredible. In short, we feel that V. Sackville-West was striving to write a Realistic novel but did not understand the world of the people she tried to create. Silas is perhaps the exception; the reader understands his isolation and his anger at a malevolent God, which to Silas is symbolized by the Abbey. But, like Iago, Silas' hatred seems not altogether motivated by his misfortunes; it seems an inborn quality of the man.

Another idea that Sackville-West was fond of considering in various aspects is the question of reality: what is real—the physical world, the world of society, the realm of the mind, the sub-

conscious? Is the inner, secret world of the individual more real
than the outer world revolving about him? All the major characters in this novel present to us facets of this idea; their inner
worlds differ but are the true realities until they are destroyed
by the one great　reality: the heart of darkness within man.
Gregory's world of well-ordered machines is destroyed by his
lust for Nan. Linnet's world of science, truth, and innocence is
invaded and is nearly destroyed by the rigidity of a "moral"
society. Silas' world of hate and pride is destroyed by the love
of the two young people. The key to this story, as in *Heritage*,
is the triumph of love over hate. All of us are blind and live
in darkness until freed by the sacrificial atonement which can
be achieved only by loving.

III   Grey Wethers

Grey Wethers (1923), the last of Miss Sackville-West's early
novels, is, in many ways, the most successful. Again we are
presented with her favorite concepts—the force of nature, the
persistence of inherited traits, the *reality* of the spirit, the all-
encompassing power of love—all these elements are blended to
form a Romantic novel of considerable poetic beauty. Like
Heritage, *Grey Wethers* belongs to the Romantic tradition
of the late nineteenth century, and it certainly bears the
stamp of the novels of Thomas Hardy. Its setting is of even
greater import to the plot than is that of *Heritage*; for, as in
Hardy's novels, the countryside performs an active role in both
plot and characterization. The setting, a village called King's
Avon, is surrounded by ancient Roman earthworks which
enclose the village; and the village is located in a hollow flanked
by the Downs and by the chalky cliffs of Wiltshire, on the face
of which is to be seen the old carved White Horse. The story
opens with a festival, held by the young people of the village,
who every ten or fifteen years scour the face of the great White
Horse. We meet the villagers: Peter Gorwyn, who is in charge
of the festivities, and Daisy Morland, who is in love with Nicolas
Lovel, a mysterious gypsy-like figure who has an invalid mother
(believed to be a witch) and a simpleton brother, Oliver.
The only gentry in the neighborhood are the scholarly gentleman Mr. Warrener, his seventeen-year-old daughter Clare,

and another somewhat mysterious bachelor of fifty, Mr. Richard Calladine. Clare, wanting to observe the festivities of the young folk of the village, rides to a clearing on the Downs. While she is observing the games and the frolicking, she is interrupted by Mr. Calladine, who takes her away because he believes the antics of the peasants unsuitable for her to watch; and she reluctantly leaves. Actually, Clare had gone to see the festival in the hope of meeting Nicolas Lovel, whom she has known since childhood. They have been in the habit of meeting, as if by chance, on the Downs; she has helped him to shear sheep, to fish, to gather osiers, and to perform all the tasks of the farmer and shepherd. Nicolas earns a living as he may, picking up odd jobs—carpentry, shepherding, mowing—wherever he can. Thus he supports his mother and brother. A lonely, silent man, he and Clare have found in each other the essential qualities of comradeship—a mutual, instinctive understanding based on their love for the countryside, the out-of-doors.

Nicolas realizes the barriers between them: they come from different classes, and he has a heritage that precludes child-begetting. On the day of the scouring of the White Horse, Oliver finds Daisy Morland alone; and, filled with desire for her, he has intercourse with the young woman, who is not averse. But she uses the situation for her own purposes; desiring Nicolas, she goes to him, crying that his "idiot" brother has begot her with child—and, therefore, in order to make her respectable, to enable her to keep her secret, and to protect his brother—Nicolas must marry her.

Perhaps Nicolas would not have consented to this marriage with Daisy had it not been that, believing he could bring Clare only grief and sorrow, he has broken with her. Clare, hurt by Nicolas' refusal to see or speak with her and not understanding his motives, seeks refuge in a union with her father's friend, Richard Calladine, who is, of course, a father-figure to the young girl. Obviously, neither Clare's marriage nor that of Nicolas can succeed. Both are completely unhappy; and their wife and husband, respectively, are driven almost to madness. (Calladine, consumed by the gloom and tragedy in their lives, actually does become mad at the end.) At length, as Daisy nears the time of childbirth, she is driven by boredom; and tells Nicolas that the child she is bearing is not Oliver's but Peter Gorwyn's,

with whom she had had intercourse a month before the scouring festival. When Oliver hears this news, he goes to Clare and
tells her that the child Daisy is bearing is neither Nicolas' nor
his own and that the real father is Peter Gorwyn. So Clare walks
out onto the Downs, meets Nicolas—and the two, now united,
disappear into the night.

The role of nature in the novel is, without doubt, the most
important one—and the most interesting. The author's strong
feeling for the English countryside is in part responsible for this
significance, but there is more; there is a oneness with nature,
a basic union of human nature with the elements. Early in the
novel Clare, who loves her native heath and the freedom of the
out-of-doors, reflects, "Tis an old, hard country; and such ghosts
as there are are bleached bones by now, dry and clean; there's no
decay about them. Why, I think that the ghosts that walk among
the stones must be as stern as the stones themselves."[11]

At first, the Downs are simply the reflection of their own natures—their youth, their joyousness, their strength. Then the
Downs become personalized—and are peopled with the tragedies
of generations of men and women: "For her, now, the Downs,
hitherto so void and so spacious under the freedom of the
winds and the cycle of the Seasons, for her now the Downs
were peopled. The dews were brushed dark with footsteps. Their
heights were scanned by searching eyes. Their flanks were
bruised by the stumble of weary limbs."[12]

The significance of nature is well illustrated and symbolized
by the two main characters in the story. Of Nicolas, the author
tells us that, when he had got the better of the Downs, he had
"got the better of his own soul." "His physical and mental endurance were alike strong enough to cope with the utmost
rigours that nature and fate were able to devise for his trial."[13]
In sum, then, nature becomes the proving-ground, the vehicle
of fate, by which man is tested. For Clare, the Downs are her
teacher, her mentor; they mature her and turn her from girl
to woman. In the happy days of youth, with Nicolas at her side,
she had always met the call of nature, the physical; later, she
accepts the call of humanity, the moral: "Out there, she could
respond, she could feel, she could learn. Once she had not wanted
to learn. She had shirked knowledge. Now, she had acquired
knowledge, and could bear a yet deeper learning. She was avid,

indeed, for the deepest draught of knowledge. Those bare great Downs, they were not bare; they were peopled. She might learn the first lesson from their storm, and the ultimate lesson from their serenity."[14]

Finally, Clare sees herself and Lovell as a part of nature, as indeed essences of nature: "They had the Downs as a bond between them; the Downs, and all nature, of which Lovell seemed the spirit, the incarnation. He was the Darkness of the Downs, their threat, their solitude, their intractability; she was their light, their windiness, their sunlit flanks, their springiness of turfs. United, they formed a whole."[15] And so light and dark, day and night, man and woman—all the dualities, the opposites—merge into a unity, a oneness, to find completion; and the catalyst is nature.

Surely the influence of Hardy is again inescapable in the force of nature, in the portrayal of country folk and customs, and in the irrevocability of fate. But an even greater influence, it seems, in this concept of nature is Wordsworthian; for the characters pass through the three stages so explicitly stated by Wordsworth: first, the physical or animal delight; second, the moral effect of nature, hearing oftentimes "the still sad music of humanity"; finally, and third, the spiritual, the mergence of a personal identity with the larger life-force of the cosmic. In *Heritage,* fate is in the genes, in inherited traits; in *Grey Wethers,* fate is the energizing force that pervades everything—the omnipresence that creates the oneness between man and nature. V. Sackville-West's concern with this force within us and around us— an idea at the base of all three of these novels—is best expressed in her own words, a passage from *Heritage*:

How trivial, how easily ignored are facts, when one's quarrel is with the enigma of force at the heart of things! It isn't often in this civilized life of ours that one comes into contact with it; one's business lies mostly with men and women whose whole system of philosophy is inimical to natural, inconvenient impulse. It obeys us as a rule, like a tame lion doing its tricks for the lion-tamer. A terrifying thought truly, that we are shut up for life in a cage with a wild beast that may at any moment throw off its docility to leap upon us! We taunt it, we provoke it, we tweak its tail, we take every advantage of its forebearance; then when the day comes for it to turn on us, we cry out, and try to get away into a corner. . . .

Something there is we don't understand: that is what frightens us,
from the child alone in the dark to the old man picking at the sheets
on his deathbed.[16]

IV   Conclusion: Learning the Novelist's Craft

Although all three of these novels exhibit qualities of a first-
rate novelist and are, in some ways, masterful, they nevertheless
are experimental ones. V. Sackville-West is learning the craft
but, at the same time, is revealing some natural proclivities that
will become, as it were, earmarks of a Sackville-West novel. In
all three novels, the setting is of more than ordinary significance; the plots, though incredible and melodramatic, are well-
contrived and structured; the mood and tone are highly Romantic and intense. All three novels seem, however, exaggerated
both in action and characterization.

In all three novels, the setting is significant, although, as we
have seen, it is most essential in *Grey Wethers*. In the *Heritage*
there are beautiful descriptive passages; the Kentish countryside
that surrounds Knole and was so great a part of V. Sackville-
West's own youth is depicted with loving care. But, as Elizabeth
Drew has observed, nature in this novel is passive; it furnishes
the fitting background for the folk-characters in the novel but
does not play an active part in the action.[17] Not so, however,
in *Grey Wethers*; for in it nature, as we have seen, is the most
potent force in the action and in the characterization. Again,
the reader admires the vivid descriptions of the Downs, of
the English folk-festivals, of the immensity and power of the
mystic force of nature. Finally, the setting of *The Dragon in
Shallow Waters*, although of an entirely different kind and
handled in a totally different manner, is no less important to the
action; but the treatment is symbolic. The Abbey at one end
of the town and the factory at the other represent two opposing
forces: spiritualism versus materialism. And the heath in which
Silas Dene tries to hide symbolizes the wasteland in Silas' own
soul. The gloom of the setting does more than reflect the mood
of the characters; it seeps into their being, and men and nature
merge. Surely V. Sackville-West seemed to have understood,
from the beginning of her career, the functions of setting.

And the author shows that she can build plot, can make the

reader participate in the action, and can create suspense. In handling these elements, she is already a master novelist. The reader persists in order to discover "how it all turns out," and there is plenty of action, for this author can tell a good tale. But even more important is her use of chance or fate; like Hardy, V. Sackville-West was deeply interested in the concept of a mystic, natural force of which man is a part, whether he will or no. This idea furnishes a base not only for these novels but also for the "transition" novels discussed in the next chapter. In all three of the experimental novels, the course of the plot is deflected by fate, of which the characters are victims. There is, however, an obvious difference between Hardy's concept of external fate and V. Sackville-West's. In her works, fate is equally *within* the character—a trait inborn that seems to be beyond the control of the individual. It remains one of the great mysteries: is it inherited through the genes (*The Heritage*); is it a god-like spirit or consciousness that is manipulating mankind (*Grey Wethers*); or is it the expression of evil inherent in human nature (*The Dragon*)? This concept of fate is, of course, not only important to plot-structure but also to characterization. In these experimental novels the characters seem, for the most part, unreal and shadowy; for the author sees them in the abstract, and they are obscured by the mists of her Romantic idea of nature.

The unreality of the characters also stems from the problem of dialogue. In *The Heritage* and in *Grey Wethers*, there is relatively little dialogue; the story unfolds through narrative. And, as we have seen, the structure of the first novel is made unnecessarily complicated by the fact that the three different techniques of narration are employed. When the characters do talk in dialogue, they employ a rather quaint, bookish English with a nineteenth-century flavor. The characters in *The Dragon in Shallow Waters* use a kind of dialect designed to show a lack of formal education and cultural background. The result in all three novels is an artificiality which makes us conclude that the author did not know these people, that they are not drawn from life.

In style, these novels demonstrate that V. Sackville-West had already developed a secure facility in the use of language and an original style of expression. Her experience in writing poetry undoubtedly trained her ear to catch and express prose rhythms and word-color. Her style generally is simple but clear and sinewy. We cite, for example, this single sentence from *Grey Wethers*: "The dews were brushed dark with footsteps."[18] Occasionally, she is carried away by rhetoric, as in the passage we have quoted from *The Heritage*. As Virginia Woolf observed, "One wonders what she means."[19] when V. Sackville-West is carried away by the sound of words. But in even the final sentence of this passage Sackville-West reins herself in and illuminates the idea with a clean, poetic image.

Although all three qualities—setting, plot, and characterization—are essential to a good novel, characterization must come first; for action and mood must develop from the character. At this point in her carer as a novelist, V. Sackville-West had all the equipment necessary to be one except understanding of her characters. But she had learned by now what all novelists must know: fictional characters must be drawn from life, from people whom the author knows first-hand. Henceforth, she portrayed characters from the English aristocracy, a class she knew well; and she found her true *métier*.

CHAPTER 7

Transition: The Dark Novels

"Oh, God! the appalling loneliness of us all."
V. Sackville-West[1]

WHILE Sackville-West was moving from the novel of the country towards the sophisticated Edwardian novels, she wrote some fiction in which she explored new settings, new techniques, and new character types. These novels are but partly successful, for in them the new *milieu* into which she was moving was only partially realized. However, they contain interesting ideas and again reveal much about her own feelings and convictions. I label them the "dark" novels because they are all concerned with the struggle of the *id*, of the subconscious, for domination of the ego. And they are all concerned with the "heart of darkness" theme—the evil deep within man.

I Challenge

Challenge (1923) has a curious literary history, for it was withdrawn from publication in England because descendants of the ancient Davenant family objected to the characters in the novel of that name; it was, however, published in the United States. What, exactly, the Davenants could find objectionable is difficult to comprehend.

This novel is strange in many ways. The setting is beautiful —Herakleion and the Greek Isle of Aphros; the water sparkles in the warmth of the sun, and the islands are outlined in sharp-edged brilliance. But the setting is in deep contrast to the tragic darkness of the plot. Young Julian Davenant, son of William Davenant (a former mayor of Herakleion), who rebels against his father's and the old British imperialistic concept of politics

91

to fight for the freedom of the islands, becomes the leader of the
Greek rebellion and is ably supported by a Greek singer Kato
(Anastasia). These two are passionately dedicated to the principle of freedom; but Julian loves Eve, his cousin, who does not
understand his devotion to the cause of liberty and who is
capable only of loving the man Julian and herself. In fact, she is
jealous of Julian's love of the islands, of his political convictions,
of his admiration for Kato. Eve, a type of woman often found in
Miss Sackville-West's novels, has early in life formed a rigid code
for herself—a definite philosophy of life. Behind an appearance
of expansiveness, of amiable sociability, lies a fundamental
secrecy that she has cherished—a secrecy that she uses both
as a shield and as a weapon. Perhaps pride is at the base of this
self-concealment, this reluctance to reveal the "true" self. This
aloneness of every individual is expressed by Julian; when he
hears of the suicide of Father Paul, who loved Eve, he cries out,
"Oh God! the appalling loneliness of us all!"[2] We cannot fail to
perceive in Eve something of V. Sackville-West herself—this
cherished feeling for the inviolability and impenetrability of
the personality.

But, to return to the plot, Eve persuades Julian to take her
to Aphros. The rebellion is at first successful; Julian becomes
president of the archipelago of islands; and Aphros prepares
for a siege. Here Eve and Julian become lovers and live in
perfect ecstasy until Eve's jealousy of Kato and lack of understanding of the importance of Julian's political career break the
spell. Malteios, a crafty former mayor of Herakleion, persuades
Eve, by playing upon her jealousy, to betray Julian and the
islanders. When the forces of Herakleion take over, Julian learns
of Eve's trickery and leaves her. Appalled by what she has done
and cognizant now of the mortal wound she has inflicted upon
Julian, Eve forces her lover and Kato to escape in the boat
originally furnished by Malteios for Eve and Julian. After making her sacrifice in expiation of her sin, she commits suicide by
drowning.

Eve is surely the best realized character in the novel. As
usual, V. Sackville-West's finest character creations are the
women; for she understood and had studied the feminine mystique. Also, her woman characters contain something of herself and generally express ideas close to her own heart. The

following passage, for example, presents Eve's basic personality problem (one also characteristic of Shirin in *The Dark Island* and, to a lesser degree, of Evelyn in *Family History* and of Lady Slane in *All Passion Spent*): "Already in her surprisingly definite philosophy of life, self-concealment held a sacred and impervious position. Secrecy—and her secrecy, because disguised under a superficial show of expansiveness, was the more fundamental, the more dangerous secrecy she recognized as being both a shield and a weapon."[3] Eve is secretive not because she is afraid of being hurt but because of her pride and her independent spirit. She truly loves Julian and is strong enough to commit suicide when she knows that her love has all but ruined him and when she concludes that she would always be a curse to him. In short, the reader understands Eve; there is no vagueness of motivation here as there seemed to be in the case of Ruth in *The Heritage*.

Contrast is neatly achieved in V. Sackville-West's portrayal of the two female characters. In appearance, Kato (Anastasia) is the opposite of the lithe, graceful, lovely Eve; for Kato is almost as broad as she is tall, is positively ugly, and is angular in her movements. The women are friends, however, until Eve becomes jealous of the singer's influence over Julian; and, when Kato learns that Eve has ruined the attempt of the Islanders to achieve liberation, she is relentless in her condemnation. Even Julian is compassionate when he sees Eve's real contrition, but not so Kato. She is also in love with Julian, but she knows that he would never love her; furthermore, her soul is devoted to the cause of liberty for the islands. This contrast between the women is emphasized near the end when Kato learns that Eve had betrayed the cause: "'Why didn't you trust yourself to me, Julian, my beloved,' she cried; 'I wouldn't have treated you so, Julian; why didn't you trust yourself to me?' She pointed at Eve, silent and brilliant in her coloured shawl; then, her glance falling upon her own person, so sordid, so unkempt, she gave a dreadful cry and looked around as though seeking for escape."[4]

In construction, this novel is simple and direct. The plot is unfolded by the all-seeing narrator, and suspense is sustained until the close. At the beginning, we wonder if Julian will choose the life of ease, the life society expects of him; or if he will

accept the leadership of the revolutionaries and fight for freedom for the ill-treated islanders. In this situation lies the challenge and also the source of conflict between generations:
Julian's father and uncle represent the established, imperialistic, mercantile interests of British colonialists; Julian embodies
the ideals of freedom, of non-conformity. He gives voice to
this struggle in a visit to Kato, and his words are those of any
young idealist of any age and time:

One instinctively opposes authority. One struggles for freedom. Why?
Why? What's at the bottom of that instinct? Why are we, men, born
the instinctive enemies of order and civilization, when order and
civilization are the weapons and the shields, we, men, have ourselves
instituted for our own protection. . . . Why do we fight against
government? Why do I want to be independent of my father? . . .
What's this instinct of wanting to stand alone, to be oneself, isolated,
free, individual? Why does instinct push us towards individualism,
when the great well-beng of mankind probably lies in solidarity?[5]

Julian finds the answer when he makes his choice and becomes
his own man. In a few months, he matures.

However, the beauty of the book lies not in the characterizations but in the setting and mood. Sackville-West has caught the
"feel" of Greek culture, of the appeal of an island world, of the
Mediterranean Sea. Here her love of nature stood her in good
stead; she pictures the setting as a painter would—with an eye
and mind alert to every detail. So involved does she become
with these scenes that she frequently indulges in lengthy descriptions. Indeed, the style is ornate, decorative; but there are
lovely passages where the author makes us "see" the picture
as vividly as if we were there. In this example, we should also
notice her use of similes:

The village hung sheerly over the sea, the faces of the white houses
flat with the face of the brown rocks, the difference in colour alone
betraying where the one began and the other ended, as though
some giant carpenter had planed away all inequalities of surface
from the eaves down to the washing water. The fleet of fishing boats,
their bare, graceful masts swaying a little from the perpendicular
as the boats ranged gently at their moorings with the sigh of the
almost imperceptible waves, lay like resting sea-gulls in the harbour.[6]

And, finally, we cite a descriptive passage which presents so well the theme of aloneness, of isolation, which the island symbolizes:

The sea, today of the profoundest indigo, sparkled in the sun below, and between the sea and the foot of the mountains, plainly, as in an embossed map, stretched the strip of flat cultivated land where he could distinguish first the dark ilex avenues, then the ribbon of road, then the village, finally the walled plantation which was his uncle's garden.... Herakleion was hidden from sight, on the other hand, by the curve of the hill, but the islands were visible opposite ... there was something symbolized in their detachment from the mainland—in their clean remoteness, their isolation; all the difference between the unfettered ideal and the tethered reality.[7]

II   Seducers in Ecuador

Sackville-West's next novel, *Seducers in Ecuador* (1925), is the one Elizabeth Drew calls "that strange little allegory."[8] Dedicated to Virginia Woolf, the novel has a fine irony reminiscent of that author's own style. The story, a kind of "ship-of-fools" one, concerns four characters on a yachting trip who become involved in the flow of their lives; yet three of them, obsessed by a delusion, view "reality" (or what the world casually labels such) through their own distorted lens. They live with their individual delusions; the consequence is that their values of life are distorted and that each lives within his own tower, alone and untouched by reality. For example, Miss Whitaker suffers from the delusion that a man in Ecuador seduced her. The author is saying that our illusions distort and discolor all life's experiences, hence the title.

The chief character, Arthur Lomax—who is, by the way, the only character with a first name—is invited to go on a cruise in the yacht of Bellamy, a fellow club-member. Lomax does not know Bellamy well, but he accepts the invitation because, since the woman he loves has married another man, he is glad to leave London. He meets the other members of the party, a Miss Whitaker, and Artivale, a research scientist. In Egypt, Lomax learns to wear colored glasses, and he becomes so enthralled with the new world he has thereby discovered that he buys all kinds of colored lens—rose, blue, black; but black

lens become his favorite. (The black ones symbolize the dis-
astrous consequences of his illusion.) Now his concept of life is
completely changed: under the influence of his spectacles, he
is removed from realities and is happy in his own illusory
world. Now his instincts prevail, and he is catapulted into action
before he thinks. Finally, he dares not remove his glasses at all;
he cannot bear the idea of returning to the "real world."

During the cruise, after Lomax finds Miss Whitaker sobbing
because she had been betrayed by "a man from Ecuador,"
Lomax, out of chivalry, marries the dejected lady. When a severe
storm arises one night, Bellamy, who seems to have enjoyed
fighting the storm, calls Lomax into his cabin to announce that
he is dying of a dread disease and that, when the time comes,
he wants Lomax to administer a poison. Since Bellamy says
that he is too great a coward to do the deed himself, Lomax
chivalrously promises to give him the lethal dosage. By now
it is obvious that our "hero" is a Don Quixote type of character.

Back in England, Lomax is summoned by Bellamy, administers
the poison—and then learns that Bellamy has willed his entire
fortune to his murderer. Lomax, knowing that he has only a
little time before he will be arrested, travels to Paris to seek
Artivale in his laboratory. Lomax reveals the whole truth and
announces that he is willing his money (once Bellamy's) to
Artivale for the sake of science. Now Lomax, still wearing black
glasses, is captured; but, at the trial, he is not permitted to
wear them; consequently, he is completely bewildered by the
"real world" and can make no defence. But he derives some
satisfaction from the three "good" deeds he has done: he has
saved Miss Whitaker from disgrace, he has rescued Bellamy
from an agonizing death, and he has left Bellamy's money to
science. Ironically, the trial proves that Miss Whitaker was never
seduced and that Bellamy (as evidenced by a postmortem)
never suffered from a malignant disease. Lomax, who is sen-
tenced to be hanged, goes to his death secure in the belief that
the last of his good deeds still prevails. But the final irony is
that Bellamy's two maiden aunts contest the validity of the
will—and win their case; consequently, the money never goes to
further the cause of science.

Significantly, Artivale, the scientist, is the only "normal"
character in the novel; he sees life as it is and escapes the de-

lusions that obsess the other characters. As the representative of science, he remains objective, uninvolved, and undeterred by fears or anxieties. For example, when Lomax, drawn to the exuberance and cheerfulness of Artivale, tries to tell him about the wonderful world of colored glasses, Artivale tries the spectacles, is amused, and then dismisses the whole idea. Perhaps the matter-of-factness of his personality saves him, for he alone "survives" in the cruise of life. The others succumb to the "mind-forged manacles" of society and to their personal delusions.

In this novel, Sackville-West adopts a technique new to her. The novelette (for it is short) proceeds in straightforward fashion; there is no introspection into the action of the characters, no attempt to explain what motivates them; and the brisk pace of narration permits little description and exposition. The novel has the quality of a well-knit detective story. Like Artivale himself, the author remains objective and detached from her characters. Her style has a clinical coolness and cleanliness that give the novel an astringent quality. Even her vocabulary and sentence structure have a detached, intellectual quality. A good example is her method of introducing the characters at the beginning of the novel: "It is now time," she writes, "to be a little more explicit on the questions of the companions of Lomax. Perhaps Miss Whitaker deserves precedence, since it was she, after all, who married Lomax. And perhaps Bellamy should come next, since it was he, after all, for whose murder Lomax was hanged. And perhaps Artivale should come third, since it was to him, after all, that Lomax bequeathed his, that is to say Bellamy's, fortune."[9] This extract illustrates the unusual style in which parallelism and repetition are the chief devices that make the sentence structure formal and artificial.

III   The Dark Island

The Dark Island (1934), although it does not belong in date of publication to this period, does belong in spirit with the other novels. Indeed, we find in this novel the ultimate expression of the author's pessimism and of her deep concern over the origin of evil within man. From her first published novel, *Heritage,* Miss Sackville-West probed the psychological depths of human nature in an effort to discover the origin of evil. *The Dark Island* does not present an answer, but we feel that she purged herself in it of the problem—and solved the perplexity. Having plumbed the depths of despair, she did not return to the "heart-of-darkness" theme again.

To the children of Cain that Miss Sackville-West had already created—Rawdon Westmacott in *Heritage,* Silas Dene in *The Dragon in Shallow Waters,* Eve in *Challenge*—she added in *The Dark Island* Shirin Wilson and Venn le Breton. The Wilsons, a rather ordinary middle-class family who live in Dulwich, consist of the blind father; the whining, self-absorbed mother; two sons, Paul and Roger; and a sixteen-year-old daughter Shirin, who is the center of the story. Shirin Wilson, the light of the household, is gay and very self-possessed; but she is also detached and proud. The family summers at Port Breton, and Shirin passionately loves the sea. Not far off-shore is the small island of Storn, and one side of it always appears to Shirin to be sunny; the other, dark and forbidding. Every year she has told herself that she will explore this dark, mysterious world; but she is afraid; something warns her not to hurry. Obviously, the island symbolizes the duality of human nature; and the attraction of the "dark" side for Shirin symbolizes her desire for isolation, for "escape" from the responsibilities of society and from reality.

One day, while on the beach, she meets a young boy about her age who is mending fish-nets. Though both of them are shy and distrustful of each other, they at length become friends. After Venn eventually tells Shirin that he lives on the island, he rows her there; and she has lunch in the old castle with Madame le Breton, Venn's grandmother. The old woman and the young girl are attracted to each other; Madame tells her that Venn is the heir to the island and to the ancient Le Breton name. Venn, a strange boy, is moody and half-uncivilized; but Shirin also has her "dark" side. A proud, independent spirit, she early in life had learned to keep her inmost self secret and untouched by the events of life. Instinctively, she feels that life is cruel—that fate, just for mischief, may take away the things a person loves the most. Loneliness is not too great a price to pay for her independence or spirit, she feels; but "nobody, she thought, can get into one's mind, if one is sufficiently determined to prevent them. Admission is by privilege, not by compulsion. Only to the person I love, if ever there is one. . . . I don't understand that thing called love, still less that thing called intimacy; I don't even want to understand it; since it apparently robs one of all independence."[10] In this last sentence, Sackville-West tells us Shirin's weakness and the cause of her tragedy: she cannot love another human being because she refuses in her pride to surrender her independence; the mystery of her being must remain inviolate.

After the death of Mr. Wilson, the family does not return to Port Breton; and Shirin meets and marries Miles Vane-Merrick, M.P. (the lover of Evelyn Jarrold in *Family History*). By him, she has three children; the oldest one, Luke, is an idiot and perhaps therefore her favorite. The marriage does not last; and, after the divorce, Shirin, who is gaining a reputation for being a hard, pleasure-seeking divorcée, again meets Venn. After they marry and go to Storn to live, Venn tells Shirin that the island is not—and never will be—hers; it belongs only to him. Perhaps he senses that she married him because of her love of Storn, not of him. Immediately, something inside of Shirin dies; all feeling for him is killed. Venn tries to break her spirit, to conquer her; but he cannot. In the course of years, they have two children—a boy, Dominic, who is like his father; he will inherit Storn. The daughter is never a character in the novel.

In time, Shirin asks her only friend, the sculptress Cristina, to come to live with her as her secretary. Once in a while Shirin goes to London to visit her children by her first marriage; but, except for these visits, she never leaves Storn. Venn becomes more and more morose and brutal towards his wife, who remains kind but aloof; and he cannot penetrate her armor. When Cristina sculpts a head of Venn, she shows that she understands him: it reveals his cruelty, his anger. Venn now turns his hatred upon her, and he is jealous of the intimacy of the two women. Knowing that the best way to hurt Shirin is to destroy this friendship, he plots the death of Cristina. One afternoon, he takes Cristina sailing and leaves her on Gull Rock, which at high tide is completely inundated. When Cristina is reported drowned, Shirin knows the truth—that Venn had murdered her; and Shirin "dies a second death": the first one had occurred when Venn took Storn away from her; the second, when he took Cristina.

Shirin still says nothing, and silently she goes about her tasks. But Venn, disintegrating because he cannot endure Shirin's strength and her fatalistic calm, develops consumption and is terribly afraid of death. The doctor tells Venn that he must go south for the winter; for a cold or pneumonia will kill him. Venn plans to go to Davos and, of course, insists that Shirin accompany him. On the eve of their departure, Shirin develops a high fever and sore throat; and as she is writing Venn a note to tell him not to come near her, he enters her room. She jumps away from him—an action he misinterprets. He thinks that he has at last caught her off-guard and accuses her of hating him. Shirin then calls him to her, kisses him on the mouth, and pretends to love him. In a few days, Venn, having caught her infection, falls ill and dies. Shirin lingers only a few weeks—and then she too dies.

The relationship of husband and wife in *The Dark Island* is reminiscent of the situation in *Heritage*. Like Ruth Pennistan, Shirin finds strength and courage to endure the cruelties of the man; it is he who breaks, who cannot withstand the silent reproach and constant reminder of his guilt. But, unlike Ruth, Shirin dies a tragic death because she is not redeemed by love. Venn and Shirin, two children of Cain, destroy each other.

The Dark Island is indeed an unpleasant novel, but it is well done. The characters are well portrayed—especially Shirin; for Miss Sackville-West's study of this attractive, intelligent woman who could not love, who could not lose herself to find herself, is convincing. The vividness of this characterization is greatly helped by the author's device of italicizing soliloquies—a device which is used sparingly but effectively. Also the sinister mood is strongly projected and sustained throughout. With this "darkest" of the dark novels, Sackville-West seems to have concluded that evil in human beings must be acknowledged; and the only resolution that she presents is that man must wrestle with this evil, must acquire a stoicism to endure evil, and, finally, must conquer evil by love. Without love, the human being cannot survive. To help him obtain the stoic endurance necessary for survival, man must turn to nature and submit to the mystery of life. Only those who are strong enough to endure the human tragedy and who are courageous enough to love freely, regardless of the cost, can triumph.

IV *Conclusion*

We have already noted that these three novels contain the same thesis: the presence of the "heart of darkness" in man's nature. However, they are of special significance to the student of the history of the English novel because they employ new devices and techniques; and they are psychological novels. They disclose more clearly than do any of V. Sackville-West's other novels the influences of the Bloomsbury Group and of Virginia Woolf. As we review these techniques employed in these three novels, we find *Challenge* an interesting study in contrasts. We have already noted the contrast in the presentation of the two major women characters, Eve and Kato; but there is also a contrast between the sexes, for we are constantly aware of the difference between the male and female viewpoints. The novel also presents the conflict between the old, imperialistic ideology of William Davenant and the youthful idealism of his son, Julian. But the contrast which we remember most vividly after reading the book is that between the bright gaiety of the Mediterranean landscape and the dark tragedy in the hearts of the characters.

Seducers in Ecuador is almost pure symbolism, and it is also a study in irony, which is employed relentlessly throughout. So non-representational is it that the characters have no "reality," nor were they intended to have. And Miss Sackville-West's style in this novel is most appropriate for her artistic purpose: the sentences are short but artfully contrived; and her diction is sparse, abrupt. There are, obviously, no descriptions to speak of; the setting could be any place, at any time. The piece is a tour de force, full of pyrotechnics, far removed from the naturalistic type of novel which was the normal *métier* of Miss Sackville-West.

Finally, *The Dark Island* (probably the best constructed novel of the three) owes more to the stream-of-consciousness technique than any of her other novels. Although all of the characters in this books are disturbed, maladjusted individuals, we empathize with them and find them unforgettable. Shirin and Venn, two passionate children of Cain, act out their tragedy against the backdrop of the Isle of Storn; and, as a result, we see the theme of the "heart of darkness" both in the microcosm

and in the macrocosm. Sackville-West's handling of this symbolism is what makes the book noteworthy.

In a sense these three novels act as a foil to the early "country" novels, for they reveal to us how far Miss Sackville-West
had progressed in the mastery of her craft and how far she
had matured towards resolving philosophical problems raised
in the early works and towards understanding herself.

CHAPTER 8

The Edwardian Novels

> "She had been sickened by the ostentation of
> life at Knole during her childhood, feeling it
> to be a betrayal of the house, and she came
> to despise what she had no wish to share."
> —Sir Harold Nicolson[1]

VICTORIA Sackville-West's best-known works are two of
the three "Edwardian" novels, *The Edwardians* (1930)
and *All Passion Spent* (1931). Both of these novels belong to a
very happy, productive period of her life; for no sooner was the
manuscript of *The Edwardians* sent to the publishers than she
was earnestly at work on *All Passion Spent*. Apparently, she
started work on it in April or May, 1930, at which time she was
broadcasting regularly for the British Broadcasting Company
and spending her leisure at Long Barn or at Sissinghurst. In
August, the family took a vacation to Italy at Portofino; and
there Vita wrote much of *All Passion Spent*. But its composition
seemingly took close to a year, for her husband wrote in his
diary on March 15, 1931, that "I read her novel *All Passion Spent*
—a lovely book."[2] Oddly enough, Harold Nicolson did not rank
very high either *All Passion Spent* or *The Edwardians*. Although
The Edwardians was written first, it and *Family History* (1932),
the last of the Edwardian novels, should be read almost as one.
For this reason, this discussion starts with *All Passion Spent*,
instead of treating it in its normal chronological order.

I All Passion Spent

The plot of *All Passion Spent*, whose title comes from the last
line of Milton's *Samson Agonistes*—"And calm of mind, all passion spent"—is simple; in fact, it is hardly a plot at all. Henry
Lyulph Holland, first Earl of Slane, dies at the age of ninety-

four, leaving his widow, aged eighty-eight. Her children, an
ill-assorted and generally disagreeable group (except for the two
unmarried ones), try to dispose of their mother's life; but she
dismisses them. After selling the town house and tossing her
jewels to a greedy daughter-in-law, Lady Slane departs to Hampstead, where she rents a house she has long admired because of
its grotesquerie. Its ancient owner is Mr. Bucktrout, an eccentric
in the Dickens tradition. Here Lady Slane lives alone, except
for her devoted French maid, Genoux.

Through flashbacks, as Lady Slane reviews her life in retro-
spect, we come to know her. When a young girl, she cherished a
secret ambition to become an artist; and, as she painfully learns
what is expected by society of a young lady from a wealthy,
aristocratic family, she ardently wishes that she had been born a
boy. Beautiful but shy, she catches the eye of a young Henry
Holland, a diplomat ambitious to advance in his world. So she
is caught; when she tells her future husband of her ambition to
become an artist, he smiles indulgently but makes a flippant
reply to the effect that she will soon be too busy as a wife and
mother to do any painting—except, perhaps, for an occasional
watercolor. And so she becomes what her society expects of her.
She assumes the role of the perfect wife for a public servant:
she travels; she attends and gives dinner parties; she stands at
her husband's side throughout his busy career; she manages to
bear and rear the children.

But now—after her husband's death—she is free and enjoys
her independence. One of the few visitors she admits is a friend
of her son Kay; he is an art collector, a Mr. FitzGeorge, who
remembered meeting her in India many years ago. At that time
he had guessed her secret, and now years later he reminds her
of his encounter. Still half in love with her, he spends many
an evening at Lady Slane's. He is the only person who understands this woman; he knows the intense individual who still
exists behind the façade that the world sees—and he alone has
penetrated her armor. At his sudden death, it is discovered that
he has left his extremely valuable art collection to her—not to
the National Gallery. Her worldly children are aghast, but
they are even more perturbed when Lady Slane rejects this
munificent bequest.

Near the end of her days Lady Slane is visited by a grandchild who has broken her engagement because she wants a career as a composer of music. Since no one in the family understands her, she seeks from her grandmother advice and consolation. In this emancipated young woman of another generation Lady Slane sees a reincarnation of her own girlhood, of her own hopes and aspirations, of her own rebellious spirit. She, of course, is sympathetic to her grandchild. At the close of their conversation, Lady Slane, dreaming of her own youth, passes quietly away—all passion spent.

To attempt to determine just how autobiographical this novel is is dangerous, but it is also inevitable. We see in Lady Slane something of V. Sackville-West's own mother, who in her late years bought an ugly house in Brighton, where she lived alone, having quarreled with most of her friends and relatives. She also inherited very valuable art treasures from an old friend and a bachelor-admirer. But we find also something of V. Sackville-West in Lady Slane. Both of them wished they had been born a boy and therefore free of the demands of society and of the double standard. If she had been a boy, V. Sackville-West could have inherited Knole and could have pursued a career.

Perhaps even something of Vita's marriage is suggested in this novel. At first Vita tried to be simply a good wife to her diplomat-husband; she tried to attend social functions, to interest herself in her husband's career. But the time soon came when she had to assert her own life and personality; she refused to "socialize," to play the game her world demanded of her. So she lived much alone at Sissinghurst, writing and gardening. Finally, as we have seen, her husband, at least partly to be with her, abandoned his diplomatic career and took up writing. So, by recognizing his wife's genius and respecting her eccentricities, Sir Harold Nicolson probably salvaged their marriage; in fact, he solidified it until it became one of the great literary romances.

The life of the English aristocracy as V. Sackville-West had seen it at Knole, during her childhood and early womanhood, repulsed her. She rebelled against it—a quiet rebellion to be sure but, nonetheless, a rebellion. Young Vita became shy and ingrown; she absented herself from her mother's parties, withdrew from society, and began writing. Like Jane Austen, she could examine objectively the people around her, dissect them under a microscope as if they were biological specimens. And their antics amused her, although they at times aroused her ire. Eventually, she learned to alleviate this irritation by writing satire. She singled out three dominant attitudes of society which especially annoyed her: the double standard for men and women, the superficiality and futility in the daily lives of the rich, the rigidity of conformity and tradition. These subjects appear again and again in her novels; and her own life was a non-violent protest against these "manacles of the mind." But the spirit of her satire is intellectual and objective rather than emotional. She was not moved to reform society, as was H. G. Wells.

The double standard plays an important part in the character-ization of Lady Slane. In her childhood dreams she saw her-self as a boy, thereby achieving the freedom and personal ful-fillment which she felt had been denied her. (V. Sackville-West always hated the distinctions between the sexes; whenever she was called an authoress, she clenched her fists and gritted her teeth.) When her granddaughter rebels, Lady Slane is pleased; and she sees in this new generation possibilities of an equality of the sexes, a recognition of woman. The conflict between gen-erations becomes involved, then, with this problem. Here, as in the other two novels, the young men and women are trying to secure greater freedom in their rebellion against the Estab-lishment. Needless to say, Miss Sackville-West is on the side of youth. In fact, the thesis of this novel is closely allied to this theme:

If only I were young once more I would stand for all that was calm and contemplative, opposed to the active, the scheming, the striving, the false—Yes! . . . She [Lady Slane] wondered whether this were not merely a negative creed, a negation of life; perhaps even a confession of insufficient vitality; and came to the conclusion that it was not so, for in contemplation (and also in the pursuit of the one chosen avocation which she had had to renounce) she could pierce to a happier life more truly than her children who reckoned things by their results and activities.[3]

All Passion Spent contains numerous examples of satire directed against other specific social customs and affectations. In the opening pages, which describe the death of Lord Slane, the hypocrisy of funeral ceremonies is exposed. And later we find satirization of the courtship and marriage code. When Deborah becomes engaged to Henry Holland, she is suddenly surrounded by tittering females—not only relatives but friends, dressmakers, milliners, and even a young French maid. Deborah feels that she is supposed to know what the whole thing is about, but the meaning of the mystery eludes her: "What a pother, she thought, women make about marriage! And yet who can blame them, she added, when one recollects that marriage—and its consequences—is the only thing that women have to make a pother about in the whole of their lives."[4]

Another bit of social satire, of the daily routine of the *far niente* class, is the picture of Lady Slane's daughter Carrie, who is smug, intolerant, narrow-minded, and self-righteous. Her days are consumed by such activities as attending meetings of ladies' clubs, having teas, and making calls upon the "proper" people. Her values are based upon the externals, the material world; her own spirit has long since dried and withered.

However, rigidity and conformity are the topics which touched most deeply the wellsprings of V. Sackville-West's own person. Almost all of her prose deals in some way or another with the battle of the nonconformist against society. The greatest crime is the shackling of the individual. For this reason, she disliked the bonds of matrimony, the labels pinned upon people, and the rigidities of family ties. Before Lady Slane at long last breaks free from such fetters, she had been "a lonely woman, always at variance with the creeds to which she apparently conformed."[5] Now, alone except for the companionship of a few eccentrics, she is no longer lonely; in solitude she finds strength and peace: "She had had enough, in her life, of people whose worldly status was their passport to admission."[6]

Satire in *All Passion Spent* is present in all the characterizations—even in that of the heroine herself. Lady Slane, in old age, learned to look back and laugh, as well as cry, at herself as she had stumbled ignorantly through life. But the most interesting use of satire in characterization is caricature. Miss Sackville-West, like Dickens, employs caricature in the portrayal of the eccentrics: the landlord Mr. Bucktrout, who is so particular to whom he will rent the house that he loves; Mr. Gosheron, the handyman who has the sensitivity of a poet; Genoux, the French maid, who understands her mistress so well and so lovingly; and finally,

Mr. FitzGeorge, the bachelor art collector who had a lifelong
"love-dream" of Lady Slane. And, like Dickens, V. Sackville-
West loved these creations; her caricatures are entirely sympathetic. They are nonconformists, the "rejects" of society—but
they are also the only genuine people. It is Mr. Bucktrout who
expresses the reason why society has passed him by: "The
world, Lady Slane, is pitiably horrible. It is horrible because
it is based upon competitive struggle—and really one does not
know whether to call the basis of that struggle a convention
or a necessity. Is it some extraordinary delusion, or is it a law
of life? Is it perhaps an animal law from which civilization may
eventually free us?"[7]

Structurally, these eccentrics are essential to the novel, but we
could remove them and still retain intact the main plot or idea.
And we could read the novel as a romantic, even sentimental,
character study, thereby neglecting the satire completely. But
artistically the form would collapse, for these characters furnish
the *cantus firmus* upon which the counter-point depends; without them, there would be no contrast, nothing to beat against.
In range, the satire in *All Passion Spent* goes from irony to
caricature to serious criticism of society. There is, however,
little irony; for V. Sackville-West's satire is generally direct and
broad rather than sharp and brittle, reflective rather bitter.

As the above quotations demonstrate, *All Passion Spent* contains much excellent writing. Here V. Sackville-West achieved
an almost perfect balance between her two styles: her romantic,
poetic style and her bare, detached style. The writing in *All
Passion Spent* is direct but not dry, simple but poetic and warm.
She uses only a few figures of speech. The story is told in the
third person by the all-seeing author, and the point-of-view
never shifts. The action takes place within a short space of a
few months.

The style, however, is only a tool for the structure of the novel.
By fixing the spotlight always upon Lady Slane, the author
achieves a singleness, a unity or concentration, quite unusual.
Furthermore, the concentration is never relaxed until the end.
All other characters are cast in the shade; but the mood, the
setting, is an important part of the structure. The decadence of
the Edwardian era, the disintegration of English society as the
Victorians knew it, the *fin-de-siècle* spirit, are beautifully con-

veyed, though obliquely, in descriptions such as that of the ugly house at Hampstead. One of the finest passages which evoke this mood is the following: "Weary, enfeebled, ready to go, she [Lady Slane] still could amuse herself by playing a tiny game in miniature with Mr. Bucktrout and Mr. Gosheron, a sort of minuet stepped out to a fading music, artificial, perhaps, yet symbolic of some reality she had never achieved with her own children."[8] Lady Slane epitomizes the Edwardian epoch; she embodies all of the best of that time, and her death symbolizes the end of an era. Thus V. Sackville-West achieves a structural unity remarkable for its concentration: the microcosm of Lady Slane's inner life is a manifestation of the macrocosm, the Edwardian world, which is dying; and the two are not to be separated.

Finally, it is the characterization of Lady Slane which achieves greatness for this novel. V. Sackville-West draws a portrait of a fine woman who has lived a life beautifully and fully. As Lady Slane gradually reveals herself, through the devices of stream-of-consciousness and flashbacks, we are taken inside her personality; and her feelings, thoughts, emotions are so sensitively revealed that of all the women characters V. Sackville-West created, her portrayal is by far the finest.

II The Edwardians

V. Sackville-West's best picture of the English leisure class during the early years of the twentieth century may be found in *The Edwardians* and in *Family History*. In theme, subject matter, organization, they are much alike; indeed, two of the characters, Viola and Leonard Anquetil, appear in both books. *The Edwardians* opens with a description of Chevron, an English manor-house which bears an obvious resemblance to the Knole V. Sackville-West knew in her childhood. Lucy, a widowed Duchess, is the owner of Chevron; and she has two children, Viola, seventeen, and Sebastian, nineteen. (Their names are taken from Shakespeare's *Twelfth Night,* where they are the twins who create confusion when Viola disguises herself as a boy.) In many ways, V. Sackville-West may be identified with both of these characters: Viola and Sebastian represent the female and male aspects of her own personality. And we are again reminded of Virginia Woolf's Orlando, who changes sex numerous times. Both of Lucy's children love Chevron as deeply as V. Sackville-West loved Knole, but they also loathe the hypocrisy of the society life led by their mother and her titled friends.

As the novel begins, Lucy is giving a week-end party, and all the proper socialites of the season are present. Sebastian is up on the roof, sulking; but, fascinated at the same time that he is repelled by the glitter, he descends at lunch time to join the party. Here we meet the other chief characters: Lady Sylvia Roehampton, still a beauty, although she has a marriageable daughter; the old Duchess of Hull; and Leonard Anquetil, a famous explorer, who, although an "outsider," is the "lion" of the current social season. Largely through Anquetil, Sackville-West exposes the shams and decadence of this society; through him, she expresses the satire. Anquetil suddenly realizes that these people do not want ideas; their talk is chit-chat about those in their "set," about investments, or about politics; their days are all alike, for they do the same things over and over—going to one another's houses, to Ascot for the races, to Scotland for the grouse season, and to the watering places for their health. And the thought occurs to Anquetil that society has always been this way and always will be: "If this is society, thought Anquetil, God help us, for surely no fraud has ever equalled it."[9] When Anquetil encourages the children to rebel against the stultifying effects of this society, Viola, a shy but determined young woman, is the easier to win away. She escapes and establishes herself in a flat in London; there she mingles with the Bohemian element and finds herself. (Again we are reminded of the young V. Sackville-West.) She finally becomes engaged to Anquetil.

In the meantime, her brother Sebastian has been maturing, but the procedure takes him longer. At the close of the week-end party, with which the book opens, Anquetil tells Sebastian that the life of a gentleman will stifle him; he will be poured into the mold, will conform, and will end his days in the snares of the genteel tradition. But Sebastian, who truly loves Chevron and loves being the master, the country squire, refuses Anquetil's offer to go on a two-year expedition because he has fallen in love with Lady Roehampton and is having his first affair of the heart. It is the old story of the teen-age boy learning about love from an experienced, middle-aged woman. Again V. Sackville-West is presenting us with the theme of the double standard. Everyone (including Lucy, Sebastian's mother) knows of the affair; and Lucy is quite content that her son learn about sex and women from one of her best friends. When, however, Lady Roehampton's husband discovers the liaison, he removes her from society. Lady Roehampton, of course, would rather abandon Sebastian than break the code of her class; and she therefore retires with her husband to their country estate. Appearances must be maintained.

So Sebastian learns. But he also learns from three other affairs with women beneath him in society. One of these, Teresa, the wife of a poor physician, teaches Sebastian the code of the middle-class. She refuses to culminate the affair, admitting finally that she was dazzled by Sebastian's attentions, by the splendor of Chevron, and by the glamor of high society. She discovers that she loves her husband; and marriage, she tells Sebastian, means the necessity of being true, for no one would ever speak to her if she were unfaithful. She too is bound by the code of her class. Like their betters, the bourgeoisie base their morals upon maintaining the appearance of virtue, not upon the quality itself.

Then Sebastian has a brief brush with Bohemia. Viola introduces him to the free world of the new generation—the artists, the models, and the intelligentsia of London. But an affair with Phil, who is only momentarily in love with him, proves distasteful. She not only rejects him, but he on his part cannot accept the disordered, undisciplined life of the Bohemians. (Is some of this V. Sackville-West's own reaction to Bloomsbury?)

The book ends with the coronation of George VI, and Sebastian plays his part in the ceremony. But he is disillusioned; he sees it only as a game, a hollow pageant; and during the ceremony in Westminster Abbey he suddenly realizes that he is a victim of fate—that he has been maneuvered by society into accepting his role, one for which he has surrendered his freedom. As Sebastian comes out of the Abbey, he sees Anquetil and runs to him. The explorer repeats his invitation—to accompany him on a three-year expedition; and Sebastian realizes that he must accept, for herein lies the only mode of escape, his last

chance for freedom. Sebastian knows that Anquetil is right
when the explorer says,

"Come with me, and learn that life is a stone for the teeth to bite
on. Then after three years you may come back with some sense of
proportion. Or there may be a war, by then, which will kill you off.
I've no doubt that you would behave with great gallantry; and I'll
even admit that tradition, by which you set such a store, will serve
you then in the stead of experience. In the meantime, will you come?"
"Chevron!" said Sebastian in the throes of a last struggle.
"You'll be a better master to Chevron."
"All right," said Sebastion. "I'll come."[10]

The structure of this novel is somewhat contrived. Its central
character, its "hero," is Sebastian; and his struggle forms the
plot. Viola is only lightly sketched; but she serves to reinforce
the thesis. The opening chapter, "Chevron," paints the setting;
and the characters, situations, and dialogue are presented through
the eyes and mind of Lucy. The next chapter introduces Leonard
Anquetil, and he becomes the author's mouthpiece for satire
upon the wastefulness and superficiality of the lives of upper-
class society. The next two chapters are devoted to Sylvia, Lady
Roehampton, and her family. The final scene in this part—where
George, having discovered his wife's affair with Sebastian, rips
down the façade and forces the lovers to face the truth—creates
the climax. In the next two chapters we view the aristocracy
through the eyes of Teresa. But at the same time—through the
use of irony—we see the bourgeoisie, the middle-class, in a
satirical light. These people emulate their "betters," but they are
as shackled by society and conformity as the aristocracy. Teresa,
like Lady Roehampton, is concerned not with her own conscience but with "reputation." The coronation scene, wherein
Sebastian, with the help of Anquetil, makes his escape, is in
the nature of an epilogue.

But the plot is hung upon a skeleton-structure of satire; and
the thesis of the novel is the chief subject of satire. The Edwardian era crumbled because of the decadence and the artificiality
of its *mores* and ethics, because of the emphasis upon appearance, not reality. Conformity and tradition—dead customs and
ideas—stifled all genuine emotion and thought. And V. Sackville-West shows us that this was a cancer not only of the aristoc-

racy (although this class might have been the worst offender) but of all classes. Both the bourgeoisie and the working class ape their "betters"; the same hierarchy, the same protocol and rigidity of tradition exist at all levels. Sebastian tried the most fashionable society, then the middle-class, and finally the Bohemian world; "and in all groups his plunging spirit had got stuck in the glue of convention and hypocrisy."[11] In depicting life below stairs, Miss Sackville-West comments that "the order of precedence was very rigidly observed, for the visiting maids and valets enjoyed the same hierarchy as their mistresses and masters. . . . Such small fry as underhousemaids and scullery-maids and the like were not supposed to have any feelings; they were only supposed to do as they were told."[12]

So the rigid code of society created not individuals but stereotypes. Symbolic of this effect is Teresa's comment upon viewing the society ladies at Chevron: she "marvelled at the uniformity of their appearance. . . . There was an indefinable resemblance, something in the metallic glance of the eye, the hard lines of the mouth, in the movement of the hands . . . no gale would dishevel that architectural hair."[13] Anquetil—the doer, the adventurer, the truth-seeker—is an outsider; society fears the Anquetils in the world, for they defy the *status quo*. It is through his influence that the two young people reject the code of the establishment—and rebel. And it is Viola who first forecasts the fall of the old generation as she shrewdly summarizes the ills of this society and tells her brother that "we are anachronisms already, though we may hold on for a generation or two longer."[14] Viola knows that "we are only a picturesque survival, even while we play at living still during the Wars of the Roses."[15] Viola also sees the dawn of a new era, with no place for the Chevrons and the feudal system. Surely these views are to a great extent those of V. Sackville-West; she felt, although there was "much that was dignified, traditional, and elegant" in the older order, that it had to go, "with all its absurd paraphernalia of servants and luxury."[16]

The Edwardians presents a brilliant satirical picture of society in the early 1900's. We are amused by the inscription on the title page: "No character in this book is wholly fictitious"; and we recognize the types at once and supply our own counterparts. This recognition is, of course, one of the chief objectives

of the comedy of manners. It is also true that the characterizations and events are taken from life, for V. Sackville-West
knew this class of society well. The book is a good example of
the old literary adage, "Write about life and people you know
and have experienced." Admittedly this novel is a period piece,
but it recreates this moment in time so vividly that it should
become a classic.

III Family History

Family History (1932), cut from the same cloth as *The Edwardians*, also presents a satirical view of English society in the
early 1920's. It shows us the two worlds in opposition, with the
young generation creating a new and better society. At the
same time, the novel presents the best of the old world; and the
consequent ambivalence is not only the author's but almost
everyone's reaction to change.

Oddly enough, Sir Harold Nicolson found this novel "very
competent and moving, but not exactly her type of thought."[17]
Still, the work has its own special charm. In some ways, it is
the best of the three Edwardian novels, for it is tightly knit;
we meet the main characters almost at once and follow them
closely as the plot unravels; and the resolution has the inevitability of the setting sun. Some of the minor characters are carried
over from *The Edwardians*, chiefly the Anquetils (Viola has
married Leonard Anquetil). On the whole, the characters are
sharply etched and individualized, in spite of the fact that we
recognize the types from which they have sprung.

The story is Evelyn Jarrold's. She, daughter of a country so-
licitor, married Thomas Jarrold, son and heir to the Jarrold's
fortune. Unfortunately, he was killed in World War I, leaving
his widow and one son, Dan, who is now the heir. The thesis of
this novel is the incompatibility of two worlds—and Evelyn is
caught between them. The problem is not so much the difficulty
of communication between generations, although this is part
of the trouble; it is in actuality a choice between the external
world of society and the inner world of the individual. V. Sackville-West herself once said that she had stayed too long with
the Edwardians and did not discover Bloomsbury soon enough;

like Evelyn, she wanted the best of both worlds, although, after her discovery of her real self, there was really no choice.

Family History presents three generations of Jarrolds, and the first is that of William Jarrold, founder of the family dynasty, who made a fortune in coal-mines and iron manufacture. He has three sons and a daughter: Tommy, mentioned above; Geoffrey, married, with a son, Robin, and a daughter, Ruth; Evan, unmarried and an alcoholic; Hester, spinster. Old Mr. Jarrold stands for all the values of the successful, self-made businessman. He must display his possessions: the town house on Park Lane, the country house, the chauffeur-driven Rolls Royce, the finest horses in his stable. Culture to Mr. Jarrold is only another sign of his prosperity; otherwise, it is useless. He is proud of the fact that his grandson is at Eton and can quote Virgil—but he is also a bit ashamed of it. He is not sending Dan to Eton for an education, but for manners and prestige. He likes to know that his progeny can afford to be idle; it flatters his vanity.

When we attend a ball at Chevron (presided over by the Lucy of *The Edwardians,* whose son Sebastian, a bachelor, is always away), we see the English aristocracy at play. Through Ruth Jarrold's eyes we see young healthy Englishmen who look like Viking Gods but have not a brain in their head. Secure in their patterns of life, they never question, never surmise that there are other worlds outside of theirs.

This world Evelyn Jarrold enjoys and yet ridicules. From middle-class stock herself, she appreciates the luxuries of life which money and prestige can obtain. She likes dressing-up, being admired and loved (even by her niece Ruth), and knowing her power over people. Yet she sees through the Jarrolds, knows them well, can detach herself, and observe them objectively. That there is a coldness, a hardness about her, she knows; for, once or twice when it had appeared, she had tried to subdue it. Evelyn Jarrold does not question the order of her world; she is not an intellectual, but neither is she stupid; and she sees that perhaps Dan and his friends—his generation—have a better set of values. But for her, personal relationhips are more important than social or political theories.

Evelyn meets a young man, fifteen years her junior, a Miles Vane-Merrick, with whom Ruth is in love. Dan too adores Miles; he has heard Vane-Merrick lecture at the Political Club of Eton

and believes that this young man is the leader of a new world.
Evelyn and Miles fall in love, in spite of the fact that he comes
from a different world from that of the Jarrolds. He is an intellectual, a Laborite, and a liberal; he knows art, music, poetry—
and he is writing a study of economics. Since meeting Miles,
Evelyn is all the more annoyed with the total absence of ideas,
with the heavy banter, and with the intolerant, narrow-minded
chit-chat of her relatives. To make matters worse, Ruth's un-
happiness gnaws at Evelyn; for, though it is obvious that the
girl is in love with Miles, Evelyn cannot help her. The family
Christmas party ends with the announcement of a baronetcy for
William Jarrold. The Jarrolds have now truly arrived; they
represent the Establishment.

When Evelyn and Dan spend a few days in Kent at a ruined
castle that Miles owns, the reader is reminded of Sissinghurst;
the author's description of this part of England, which she
loved so well, is beautiful. Evelyn, whose marriage had been
one of convenience, has not really known passion until she loved
Miles; she, who has had plenty of experience with men, has not
had experience with her own heart. Miles teaches Dan to love
music and Greek drama, as well as to explore ideas; and, in the
meantime, the love affair of Miles and Evelyn progresses. The
vitality and intensity of the man hold Evelyn; yet she is aware
that, although love, to Miles, is an exciting new experience for
him, it is not the be-all and end-all that it is for her: he can
separate it from the rest of his life and his being. Evelyn only
barely manages to hide her chagrin, her jealousy, towards Miles'
preoccupation with his writing, with his farming, and with his
political campaigning. But their love flourishes in the idyllic
setting of the countryside.

In London, however, with Dan back at Eton, the love affair
becomes difficult for Evelyn and Miles because to her there is
nothing but love; to Miles, there are many other facets of life,
and many other activities than love. Furthermore, the two worlds
cannot be blended; she tries but cannot really understand his
point of view, his need for a world of men. And the generation
gap adds to their difficulties. One evening, Miles takes Evelyn
to the Anquetils, who, like the Bloomsbury group that V. Sackville-West stumbled into, are the Bohemians of their day. (Leonard and Viola Anquetil strongly suggest the Woolfs.) Evelyn,

however, is out of her element. The informal studio-living room, the absence of servants, the girl in pants, the "serious" talk (these people had no chit-chat; gossip, personalities did not interest them, only ideas)—all these things disturb and anger her. But she admits that these people are real, clever—and that they care passionately for their ideas.

Finally, the break occurs when, after a violent quarrel about the Anquetils, Evelyn refuses to see Miles. Months pass, and at length Viola Anquetil suggests that Miles attempt to see Evelyn; for she has given him up for his own good, realizing that the affair cannot last because of the difference in their ages and the difference in the backgrounds. Miles drives down to Newlands, only to learn that Evelyn and Dan have gone to Spain for the summer. He returns to the Anquetils and begins going out with Lesley, their nineteen-year-old daughter, just home from the Sorbonne. But Evelyn, while in Spain, realizes that her life is over—without Miles, it is empty. She knows now that selfish love, possessive love, brings only misery. And Dan, as master of Newlands and the Orlestone Colliery, has matured and is determined to establish a model community—to build special schools, a theater, an art gallery, tennis-courts, and a swimming pool for the colliers. Then the moment comes when Dan asks about Miles—and Evelyn is surprised to learn that her son has known of the affair all along.

When she returns to London, Evelyn has a hard time escaping from Miles. His book, now out, is an important study. The newspapers are full of references to his name; the *Times* proclaims him a promising statesman. Evelyn begins to fail; she sleeps badly and can barely get through the mornings. Finally, she goes to see Viola Anquetil to ask her whether Miles and Lesley are engaged or are in love; and Viola assures her they are not. When Miles enters, Viola leaves them alone. But once more the old recriminations arise; Evelyn upbraids Miles for his negligence, and he accuses her of not caring about his career, only about herself. This quarrel ends the love affair.

When Dan goes to France, Evelyn is alone in London for the winter. One night when her brother-in-law Evan and she are dining at a restaurant, they see Miles and Lesley together at a nearby table. As she and Evan are leaving, Evelyn stops to speak to them. After leaving the drunken Evan, Evelyn goes home through a thick fog and, leaning out the window, wonders about Miles and Lesley. Finally, she goes to bed; but she awakens with a high fever. Viola Anquetil takes care of Evelyn; but, with no will to live, Evelyn does not fight the pneumonia. On the last evening of her life, Dan and Miles are by her bedside.

Unlike *The Edwardians, Family History* is not primarily concerned with satirizing the trivia, the externals, of the life of the fashionable world. However, there are some moments that offer light, satirical humor. For example, Miss Sackville-West does not use satire in describing Chevron, the estate in *The Edwardians*; but *Newlands*, the manor in *Family History,* is a different matter. The house is "new" and ugly but impressive. Like the nouveau riche, its sole purpose is to display the wealth of its owner. Its gardens are formal and artificial; everything proclaims the work of man. Then there is a satirical portrait of the fashionable physician, the rich specialist whom the nurse treats with a shade more deference than she does the family doctor. The specialist, called in consultation, changes the prescription just enough to irritate the family physician but not enough to improve the patient's health. Then the specialist drives away in his Rolls-Royce to his next rich patient.

Again, like E. M. Forster, V. Sackville-West pokes fun at the "starched conformity" of the English. Looking at the young people attending a dance, one of the characters muses, "The standard of looks was amazing; they had the distinction and beauty of thoroughbred animals. The young men were as elegant as greyhounds, the young women coloured as a herbaceous border. What did it matter . . . that these sleek heads contained no more brains than a greyhound's since those slender bodies expressed an equal grace? What did it matter that their code should strangely enough involve a contempt for the intellectual advantages which might have been theirs: what did it matter that they should immune themselves within the double barricade of their class and nationality?"[18]

Another topic of satire is one of the author's favorites—her contempt for the rituals of courtship and marriage. Miles dislikes the institution of marriage, but he would marry Evelyn if she so desires. Marriage, he declares, reminds him of Mr. and Mrs. Noah and of the animals going in two-by-two. But it is the juxtaposition of two worlds, two conflicting points of view towards life, that offers the chief material for satire. This problem is not primarily one of class, although money may tend to make the wealthy smug and powerful in the society they have set up. As did E. M. Forster (especially in *Howard's End*), V. Sackville-West has pitted the world of externals, of material values, against the world of the inner man, the world of ideas and creativity. Society upholds the materialistic standard; therefore, the non conformist is always at odds with society and finds himself the "outsider." When Evelyn visits the Anquetils for the first time and sees the "other" world, Viola tries to explain the difference. Victorianism had taught society that the better bred one was, the more tightly he was trained to shut his mind: "You were taught to be less and less an individual, and more and more of a type. And our extraordinary theory about character came in, as though character and brain and imagination were incompatible. The only kind of brain we tolerate at all, in this country, is the political brain or the administrative brain. We don't jeer at our statesmen or at our administrators as we jeer at our artists."[19]

The contrast between the two worlds is perhaps best exemplified by Dan and his grandfather. Dan is the voice of the rebellious youth. One of the causes of friction between him and his grandfather is Dan's distaste for hunting. Old Mr. Jarrold, in talking to Evelyn, puts it this way: "Tommy was a sportsman, whatever you may say. He hadn't an idea in his head, but he could get his horse over a fence as cleanly as anybody.... It's not natural for a boy of his [Dan's] age to think for himself."[20]

But Dan is most disturbed by the shallowness and the conformity of society. He thinks all his mother's friends silly: "They all slap me on the back and ask how I'm getting on at cricket, or how many days hunting I hope to get this season, or whether I'm a corporal yet in the O. T. C. . . . and am I going into the Guards or into the business? . . . . And it isn't because I'm a schoolboy, it's because those are the things they really think important. . . . Nobody seems to care about what you are, but only about what you do. . . . They don't care in the least what you are inside; and what you are inside is a thing to be rather ashamed of anyway."[21] But Dan recognizes his grandfather to be the "real thing," even though the two have different values and standards: "I like Grandpapa and Granny all right enough, but I can't stand the others. . . . Why do they sneer at all the things I like? Why does Uncle Geoffrey pull my hair and say, 'Going to be a poet, Dan?' just because I didn't have time to get it cut? Why do they think it *funny* to like poetry and pictures and music, and make jokes about them, when they're so damned solemn themselves about their golf or England's chances against Australia?" And then Dan puts his finger upon the central cause of the conflict. "Grandpapa's different somehow; it's true that he doesn't care a hoot for the things I like either, but you do feel that he's made something of his life, even though it is only business. . . . One doesn't mind his being a Philistine, exactly. But all the guts seem to have gone into him and left none over for his children."[22]

The other spokesman for the new world, Miles Vane-Merrick, views the situation from a wider perspective. The country people are dying out; their sons and daughters are moving to the city. The Establishment complains that the young have lost a sense of dignity: "It was never undignified to be content with what you truly were. Pretension only makes for falseness and vulgarity."[23] But Miles sees that the problem lies deeper: the Jarrolds and their tribe are products of Victorianism, and he paints a satirical picture of Victorian England. Like Anquetil in *The Edwardians,* Miles believes in the emergence of a better society: "They [the Victorians] believe in reputation and in respectability and in keeping up appearances . . . in condemning women to bear child after child, whether they can feed them adequately in their early years, educate them according to their talents, and settle them in after-life, or not,—all for the sake of keeping England What She Is. Give us emancipation from such ideas. . . . You Jarrolds are anachronisms today. They ought to be stuffed and put under glass."[24] These two proponents of the new generation, Dan and Miles, are inheriting the earth; the Jarrolds—and all they represent—are disappearing.

From the illustrations I have quoted, it is apparent that V. Sackville-West's satire is broad, direct, and intellectual—not sharp, subtle, irritable, or vicious; she does not employ a sabre-toothed weapon, nor does she scold. In both *The Edwardians* and *Family History* the social satire forms the structural base upon which the plot is hung. As in *All Passion Spent,* unity is achieved by maintaining the focus upon one central character. Evelyn Jarrold, like Lady Slane, is always the pivot around whom all action revolves and through whose eyes we see the other characters. V. Sackville-West understood well this type of woman—an intelligent, sensitive, mature woman of the aristocracy whose world and horizons have, however, been circumscribed by the society in which she moves.

Furthermore, Evelyn is the only character in the novel that is fully developed; all the rest are only partially realized, particularly the men. We never really know Dan and Miles, for they exist only in relationship to Evelyn. This criticism does not necessarily indicate a weakness; on the contrary, it may be a source of strength: the story is Evelyn's, and there is no shift in point of view. The tension is sustained throughout by Evelyn's struggle, her ambivalence towards the two worlds. She would have them both; and, since she cannot, the only resolution is death.

IV *Conclusion*

The three novels we have discussed in this chapter are not only V. Sackville-West's best known ones but also her finest. They have much in common: all three are set in early twentieth-century England; they draw their main characters from the English aristocracy, or upper middle class; and they satirize the lives, attitudes, and values of those from these strata of society. And all three novels present the same thesis: the destruction of the Edwardian era by a new generation seeking greater freedom for self-expression.

In form and idea, they may be classified as satirical novels of manners, with an undercurrent of sadness attributable not only to the deaths at the conclusion of Lady Slane in *All Passion Spent* and of Evelyn Jarrold in *Family History* but also to the author's own feeling of regret at the death of an era in England history. These novels belong, therefore, in the long, distinguished tradition in English letters: that of the satirical novel of manners which began with Fielding and includes Jane Austen and E. M. Forster, who seem most akin in spirit to V. Sackville-West. The tradition seems to be dying out; its gently amused tone and its nonviolent type of satire seem now to be replaced by the Swiftian type, which displays a bitter, violent disgust, a revolutionary spirit.

Critics of these novels have taken Miss Sackville-West to task on three main counts: (1) that she constructs an elaborate apparatus which leads the reader to expect a more biting satire than the author conveys;[25] (2) that she displays a lack of profundity in character interpretation;[26] (3) that she is guilty of a preciosity, a kind of literary anemia.[27] In reply to the first criticism, I believe that Miss Sackville-West intended only to laugh at the foibles of society, to ridicule the Edwardian world. Like Evelyn Jarrold, she wanted the best of both worlds. She herself told us that she wanted the best of the "Bloomsberries" and of the Edwardians. When, after World War II she witnessed the disintegration of the values and traditions which she loved, she sorrowfully turned inward to create "another world than this." The paradox of her position is perhaps best exemplified by her great love of Knole, her feeling for English history in an unbroken descent, her passion for nature and the countryside— values set against her rejection of the code of society, the sterility of the lives led by the idle rich, her sturdy resistance to the starched and rigid conformity. So Miss Sackville-West is not a revolutionary or reformer; she never preaches or advocates the overthrow of any ideology. It is true that the structure of *The Edwardians* is top-heavy for the spirit of the satire, for there she employs a wider canvas, presents more characters, and designs a somewhat elaborate setting. However, her material is always under control; and she maintains the tone of the satire —a detached, amused point of view—toward her material. There can be no question of her sympathy in *All Passion Spent* and in *Family History* with the elegant, Edwardian heroines Lady Slane and Evelyn Jarrold. But we are always mindful of the fact that these women are exceptions in their class, atypical and nonconforming.

The charge of lack of depth in character portrayal is perhaps a more damaging one; and, if the critics who made this allegation meant that Miss Sackville-West's gallery of portraits does not display a cross-section of society, a knowledge of diverse types, or that her characterizations show certain limitations, I would agree. She shows genuine understanding of women from the upper classes who are intelligent and who possess a fine awareness in personal relationships. In this area she is superb; she communicates most sensitively the thoughts and emotions of such female characters as Lady Slane. In short, V. Sackville-West understood the feminine mystique. She is not at home with the lower-class characters, nor is she always successful with the males in her portrait gallery. Anquetil in *The Edwardians* is, however, an exception.

Just as V. Sackville-West is limited in the types of characters she portrays, so is she limited in the material she employs. The charge of preciosity, of fragility, results from a misunderstanding of what Miss Sackville-West set out to do. She is not concerned with the large arena of life, the grandiose or the great ideologies. Complex characters and abnormalities do not interest her, and the only exceptions are found in *The Dragon in Shallow Waters* and *Seducers in Ecuador,* both of which deal with psychologically disturbed personalities and present violent action. She is interested in the daily lives of gentle people, in their handling of personal relationships, and in their inner worlds. And she is concerned with the problem of evil in the heart of man. Furthermore, she is adept at creating a mood, at catching an ever-present emotion or spirit. Again she can re-create an era of the past, making it live again. If this artistry be preciosity, we must accept it as a necessary concomitant of her art. But the allegation may refer as well to a quality of her style. Her descriptions are often poetic, and she is a purist in her use of language. Her characters generally talk in the best English and sound like educated, cultured human beings. Because we have become accustomed to the use of slang, colloquialisms, and solecisms in fiction, Miss Sackville-West's novels seem old-fashioned and unreal. In this respect, too, she is a "lady of the tradition."

CHAPTER 9

The Late Novels

"I wish I could sort out my ideas about this new world. I feel one ought to be able to adapt oneself, and not struggle to go back to, and live in, an obsolete tradition."

—V. Sackville-West[1]

I Grand Canyon

WITH the outbreak of World War II, both of the Nicolsons were busy with war duties. Much time was spent in broadcasts; in civilian defense work; and, for Sackville-West, in mobilization of the Women's Land Army. She, of course, was greatly concerned about the maintenance of rural country life and about stimulating interest in the planting of vegetables and crops to feed the children evacuated from the cities. In spite of these grave distractions and anxieties (Sissinghurst itself was on the direct route of the bombs for London), Sackville-West found time to write a war novel, *Grand Canyon* (1942). In its preface, the author tells us that the tale is completely fictional; it was not intended to foretell future events nor to indicate the path that civilization would take. She assumes, for artistic purposes, that Great Britain has been defeated by Germany and that the United States is trying to mediate a peace settlement with Germany but is trapped in a gigantic Nazi scheme to destroy the whole world.

The setting of the novel is, as the title indicates, the Grand Canyon and the hotel on its edge; however, the characters are international. Since the Grand Canyon was one of the two sights in America that impressed V. Sackville-West the most,[2] the setting is realistic; even the hotel pictured in the story resembles the rustic lodge of Harvey's that still caters to sightseers. The Hopi Indians furnish another realistic touch; for,

124

as the story opens, we are reminded, quite appropriately, of the Indian legend that the spirits of the dead descend into the canyon, as if it were the entrance to the underworld. So do these characters in the novel, as we shall see.

At the beginning, we meet the two main characters: Mrs. Helen Temple, an English widow, and Mr. Lester Dale, an Englishman, a bachelor, and a perpetual wanderer. But every year Dale returns to the canyon, fascinated by it; he thinks it no wonder the Indians believed that it held the secrets of life and death. Mr. Dale, always a spectator of human life, watches with amusement the antics of the visitors at the canyon and of the guests in the hotel. But he especially watches, for it pleases him, the movement of his compatriot, Mrs. Helen Temple. He sees her speak to an Indian boy, who goes galloping off at once into the Painted Desert; he sees her walking serenely along the edge of the desert, speaking to the college boys and girls coming up from a day's trip down the Bright Angel Trail. Since, nearby, there is an air force unit on manoeuvres, the girls are vacationing at the hotel.

Among these young people are a brother and sister, Loraine and Robert Driscoll; Robert, who is ten years older than Loraine, is a pilot. As Mrs. Temple paints a picture of the family life and background of these two who represent average, upper middle-class American society, Sackville-West's gift for gentle, good-humored satire shows us her point of view towards the American Philistines. As in the English novels, the young generation is creating a new world—a different one from that of their elders; they are seeking honesty, personal fulfillment, reality. They condemn the other world for its "phoniness"— and, again, the reader is reminded of E. M. Forster.

Loraine Driscoll, who is more thoughtful, more tender and aware than her companions, muses: "How odd not to know if your father is really rich or just half rich. Why do parents conceal such things from their children? Why is there always such secrecy about money? Either people boast or else they conceal; they don't seem ever to get it right. If I had money or if I hadn't money, if I were rich or if I were poor, I wouldn't mind anybody knowing about it one way or the other. I just don't understand the pretence that goes on about it one way or the other."[3]

Sackville-West also presents a contrast between the New World and the Old World—the European and the American. Mr. Dale, watching the young people dance, expresses his bitterness and European outlook:

You see, I do not like looking back on the thousands of my young compatriots who gave their lives when they were just coming into flower. . . . We suffered so much that it remains difficult for us to forgive those who didn't suffer. . . . I think the reason I am so disagreeable about these boys and girls is that they experienced our tragedies only by proxy. They didn't live in Europe, did they? They didn't see their homes bombed: they didn't hear daily about their villages being shaken down by land mines. . . . It is human nature not to mind very much about what happens three thousand miles away from where you are yourself. . . . They never knew what a blitz meant. They never saw their farm-houses ruined by craters appearing in the middle of their corn. Lucky, they were, not to live in Europe, not to live in Poland, in Rotterdam, or even in England.[4]

But the holiday spirit and bright setting are deceiving. Mr. Royer, who for two years has been manager of the hotel, is waiting for the telephone-code message from Nazi headquarters, which will tell him to set the hotel on fire, the signal for attack. On the evening when the novel begins, the message is received. But the young men in the hotel murder Mr. Royer, when he, in his moment of triumph, announces the supremacy of Naziism. At once Mr. Dale assumes command, directing the guests to gather supplies and to descend into the canyon. Just as the little group reaches the head of the Bright Angel Trail, a big crash seems to blow the rocks in the canyon, and the air shudders. This event closes the first part of the novel; and, as we learn later, this bomb killed all of the characters; for only their spirits descend into the canyon. We are not told this fact; we realize it through a series of clues: the climate does not affect the members of the party; the blind man now sees; the deaf man hears; and Sadie, the waitress, is cured of her tuberculosis.

The group of spirits reach Phantom Ranch. A radio set there keeps them informed of events in the real world. Overhead, an air battle is in progress. The radio announces that enemy attacks are being made over the United States, a serious air battle is developing over the Grand Canyon, and enemy submarines have blocked New York Harbor. On the fifth day, a young airman, shot down, falls into the canyon; he is the Frenchman, Louis, whose bride, Jacqueline, is one of the young people in the party. Louis, when he gradually enters into the immortal world, gives the others a clearer picture of what has transpired:

"After all that had happened!" he said. "After all the betrayals, the broken assurances, the secret scheming! Is it impossible for humanity to learn? Or is it impossible for us to connect any given event with its predecessors and probable successors? To observe any event, not as an isolated adventure, but as a drop in the stream of causality? It seems so. We cannot learn. Experience means nothing. . . . How impossible to express the foolishness and wrongness of this human race; how impossible to express their striving after their highest aspirations and their fall down into the lowest trough. . . ."[5]

But in the canyon the souls of the dead people now find love, peace, and beauty. The young French couple, Louis and Jacqueline, wander about blissfully in their new-found love, Loraine Driscoll finds peace and understanding of her relationship with her brother (now dead in the desert above), and Helen Temple and Lester Dale find contentment in platonic love. But, above them, the world is being destroyed by hatred, by evil. And so we have another contrast between two worlds. At the begining of the novel Mrs. Temple sent an Indian boy with a message to the "hermit," a very wise man whom she had known in Europe and who now dwells in a cave in the desert. Soon after the party reaches the bottom of the canyon, the Indian boy appears on the rim and shouts a message from the hermit to Helen Temple: "Message from Mr. Hermit. . . . He alive still. He send love. . . . He say everything all right in the end. He send love." And the last word of his message wanders around the gorge, reverberates, and echoes "love, love, love, love."[6] When a sniper then kills the Indian boy, he too joins the souls in the canyon.

The hermit may well symbolize the element of mysticism which seems to have attracted Sackville-West all her life. Here again we are reminded of the influence of E. M. Forster's novels, (this time *A Passage to India*), upon V. Sackville-West. And the Indian legend about spirits of the dead inhabiting the canyon now reminds us that this is the "other" world.

The book ends with the United States apparently losing to

an all-powerful Nazi organization. Nature reflects the disintegration by causing an earthquake in New York City and a tidal
wave along the New England coast. But, while madness and
destruction reign above them, Lester Dale voices the requiem:
"Not until she [earth] shakes this whole race off into the void
will peace return.... Is it, after all, possible that some vision
of sanity may come through the clouds, not in a miraculous
blending, but in a pervasive dawning that will bring understanding between soul and soul and peace between nation and
nation?"....[7]

And, a little like Adam and Eve at the close of Milton's *Para-
dise Lost*, Helen Temple and Lester Dale in serenity and confidence take an evening stroll along the river: "Let us go, Helen;
let us walk in this place where there is no misunderstanding.
Where there is nothing but beauty and comprehension, those
two smothered elements which hide in all souls and are too
seldom allowed to find their way to the surface. Here we are
purified. Is it indeed necessary for that man should die in order
to uncover the meaning of life?"[8]

Grand Canyon exhibits in every line and phrase the artistry
of a master-craftsman. Although not primarily a novel of character, the characters are beautifully and precisely etched. And the
structure of the novel is unmistakably clear. Part one deals with
the events in the hotel and closes with the crash that killed all
the members of the little party as they descended into the
canyon. Part two, "The Canyon," is the "other" world, where
our characters find peace and happiness while they are informed
by radio of the mortal destruction consuming the "real" world.

But perhaps the themes, or the ideas, presented most interest to the reader. They include many of the concepts of V. Sackville-West that we have already noted in her other works—the
concepts that must have lain closest to her heart. First of all, the
reader is struck by the cluster of dualities, by the opposing
"worlds" he encounters in this novel: the new (American)
world versus the old (European), the young generation versus
the old, the earthly (mortal) world versus the divine (eternal)
world. Concerning this last aspect of the novel, the reader
notices that Miss Sackville-West does not speak of God and his
Heaven; her "after-life" is instead a pagan or, better, a Platonic
existence where the body has become "all mind."

In addition, we are reminded very much of John Donne's concept of love and of his metaphysics; and this metaphysical idea leads to another one of the themes: After Helen Temple and Lester Dale have descended into the canyon and have become spirits, they share an experience which they call their "drollery." There are times when "for a few intense moments, their eyes meet; not a word is spoken, but their spirits seem to soar and unite." In considering this phenomenon, Helen compares it to the almost trancelike mood which "possessed the artist in moments of creative inspiration, the visionary on the brink of revelation, the mystic in the hour of union.... It was like a very prolonged, very quiet orgasm of the understanding instead of the quick and quickly forgotten orgasm of the senses; and it was an understanding which comprised not only their two selves, but every mystery latent in the invisible universe."[9] Thus does Sackville-West express the mysticism of the spirit, of unexplainable and inexplicable psychic phenomena of which she was always aware.

Finally, we find in *Grand Canyon* another instance of her handling of the "heart of darkness" theme. Not only is the problem of evil apparent in the macrocosm, in the dominance of the Nazi machine, but it occurs also in the microcosm, in the brother-sister relationship of Loraine and Robert Driscoll. In the "other world" Loraine is finally freed, purged of her love-hate passion for her brother. As she tries to explain to Mrs. Temple this feeling she had for her brother, she speaks of the dreadful affinity they had for each other; "curst" is the word she uses: "I hated my brother, I dreaded him, and he poisoned me. I hated him as I hope I shall never hate again; I loved him as I hope I shall never love again.... There was a streak of real evil in Robert, a streak of the real cruel devil that hurts himself in order to hurt someone else; he was a fallen angel. Poetic justice fulfilled its mission when Robert, like a falling angel, got shot down from the sky."[10] Helen Temple recalls Electra and Orestes, and she also ponders the question of reincarnation, of the origin of evil, of the mystery of the human soul.

II The Devil at Westease

For the remainder of World War II, Sackville-West wrote no fiction; and her next novel, *The Devil At Westease*, did not

appear until 1947. A very different sort of fiction, it seems to
have been written as a relief from the strain of the war years.
It is an unusual and well-told mystery "yarn"—a "who-done-it."
Written in the first person, the narrator is Sir Roger Lilliard, a
young novelist just discharged from the Royal Air Force, who
seeks peace in a quiet village in rural England. At Westease,
he purchases an old mill with a fifty-five-acre farm. The descriptions of the English countryside offer another opportunity to
the author to express her love of the land, her deep feeling for
country life. Then Roger meets the local gentry: an internation-
ally famous but eccentric painter, Wyldbore Ryan; the scholarly
old professor Warren, who lives in the Manor House; the rector
Mr. Gatacre, his invalid wife, and his daughter, Mary. She
furnishes the romance, for the two young people fall in love.

Lilliard settles down in his mill and begins work on a novel.
As time goes on, he become a frequent guest at the Rectory,
where he soon realizes that Mary is the mainstay of the family.
Her father, a frail, elderly gentleman, is "henpecked" by a
demanding self-centered wife who makes the most of her
invalidism. The Professor, too, Roger visits and likes; and the
Professor in turn grows fond of the young man, whom he considers somewhat as a son. In fact, he bestows upon Roger a
valuable Greek coin because the head on it resembles Roger;
and this coin Lilliard carries with him in a pouch as a kind of
talisman. But the artist, Wyldbore Ryan, Roger intuitively dis-
trusts. When he goes up to London and sees an exhibit of
Ryan's paintings, Roger is haunted by a sinister quality in all
of the pieces, excellent as they are otherwise.

Then, in the proper fashion of a mystery novel, Mr. Gatacre,
the Rector, is found mysteriously murdered in his study. Everyone seems to have a tight alibi, except Mary, who was supposed
to have gone to Bristol that evening but had returned home
unexpectedly because of bad weather. Lilliard, of course, sus-
pects Wyldbore Ryan; but the artist was dining with Professor
Warren that evening, according to the housekeeper, who said
that she saw Mr. Ryan and heard the Professor's voice over the
house-phone when he asked her for some wine.

With the suspicion of guilt hanging over her, Mary refuses
to marry Roger. When the Professor learns of his friend's un-
happiness, the old man disappears, leaving a note which states

that he was the killer; but no one really believes his statement. By now, Roger remembers that actually no one ever saw the Professor and Ryan together; and the fact that the fingerprints on his Greek coin are Ryan's confirms Lilliard's growing realization that the two are the same person—a Jekyll and Hyde situation. Only Roger Lilliard knows, and he confronts Wyldbore Ryan with the evidence. Ryan begs Lilliard not to betray him to the police: the case, so far as the law is concerned, is closed by the Professor's disappearance and letter. Now Roger is confronted with a moral problem: shall he turn over a criminal to the law or save a very great painter, perhaps the greatest England has ever had?

This moral problem is never solved, because, when Roger tells Mary the whole matter, she makes him confess that the story is only a fabrication—it is the novel that he has been writing:

So here, very reluctantly, and entirely against my artistic conscience, I add the required note to state that Mr. Gatacre, still happily in perfect health, continues his cure of souls as the beloved rector of Westease; that my mother-in-law is one of the most charming of women; that Professor Warren still potters delicately amongst his coins; that the splendid artist whom I have disguised under the name of Wyldbore Ryan goes from strength to strength, and that Mary and I esteem ourselves deeply honoured by his friendship. Still I sometimes wonder . . . supposing it had all really happened, what should I have done? Reader, what would you have done?[11]

The novel is not a profound one nor is it a *tour de force*; it is, however, entertaining, and the descriptions of the setting (the English village) are especially charming. The use of the doppelgänger to resolve the mystery adds interest and piquancy. We feel that the author, who without doubt fully enjoyed writing the book, probably considered it a "bagatelle."

III   The Easter Party

The Easter Party (1953), Sackville-West's next novel, again shows the sureness of technique, the calm assurance of a mature writer; but it also is a short novel (almost a novelette) with a touch of fantasy—a quality that all these late novels possess and that ranges, as we have seen, from the macabre to the mystical. *The Easter Party,* like the Edwardian novels, is concerned with the leisured life of English upper-class society. When Sir Walter Mortibois, a famous lawyer, and his wife Rose hold a house party at their country estate, Anstey, for the long Easter weekend, their guests are Dr. Gilbert Mortibois, Walter's brother, who is an eminent brain specialist; Lady Juliet Quarles, a society woman of slightly notorious reputation; Lucy Packington, Rose's sister, with her husband Richard and son Robin. And there is Summers, the unassuming but all-knowing English butler. But perhaps the most important character is Svend, a beautiful and aristocratic Alsatian dog; for the two loves in Walter Mortibois' life are Svend and Anstey. The description of this estate demonstrates once more V. Sackville-West's knowledge and love of English manor houses and their gardens. Yet, as Lucy realizes, Anstey, although a lovely rose-brick Queen Anne house set in a park of trees, is no one's home because there is no love between Walter and Rose.

When the party has gathered, Rose takes her sister Lucy to her room; and, through their reminiscences, we are informed concerning antecedents. The sisters, daughters of a minister, were reared in a provincial, middle-class home; but they are completely different. Lucy is pretty in a frowzy sort of way, not bright but very content with the life of a "normal" young girl. When they met their husbands at a tennis tournament at the neighborhood manor house, Dick Packington was just a nice young man, an extrovert, ready for love; Walter Mortibois, however, was different. Already an important authority on criminal law, he realized that he needed a hostess for London and Anstey; but he wanted no romance, no wife except in name only, and of course, no children. Believing that the tragic failure man had made of the world could be stopped only by refusing to increase the human race, he nevertheless sought to make life as comfortable and beautiful as possible. He liked fine pictures, delicious food and rare wines, books and music. Therefore he would find a beautiful woman who would be decorative, who would be an asset to him socially, and who would be evidence of his good taste.

After only one meeting, Walter asks Rose to marry him, stating the conditions of the marriage explicitly. He makes it very clear that he does not love Rose; but she accepts him on his terms. After a few months of married life she discovers that she loves him. He has given her a new set of values, a new concept of life, where people cherish fine things, live according to a well-considered philosophy and ethical code, and value human dignity and personal integrity. For twenty-three years, then, these two have lived together. Rose had had to learn never to display any emotion or any desire for love. Both of them were proud, and the world assumed that this marriage was the contented, serene affair it appeared to be. Only Walter's brother, Gilbert, had long ago guessed the truth; but he had never spoken of it. No one else even suspected Rose's virginity.

On the eve of the Easter Party, Lady Quarles (Juliet), seeks out Walter and goes for a walk with him and the dog Svend along the lake and into a little grotto. There she tells Walter about her good-for-nothing son who is in trouble, and she begs Walter to plead the boy's case. When Walter hesitates, Juliet upbraids him for his lack of warmth and human understanding. In the midst of this conversation, both Juliet and Svend suddenly go into a trance; they freeze, as if immobilized, and seem to be suffering a kind of ecstatic agony. The seizure lasts but a moment; then both the woman and the dog relax. Walter, puzzled, tries to discover the meaning of this seizure; but Juliet can only say that once or twice before she has endured this experience; it had come upon her in the country and after an emotional crisis. Once, when it occurred, she declares, she distinctly smelled the odor of a goat. Walter is disturbed; perhaps there are more things in life than his philosophy encompasses. He remembers an old judge who also accused him of lack of passion, of sympathy, and he is troubled.

When Easter morning comes, Svend, who sleeps in his master's room, wakens Walter, who romps with him in bed, then takes the dog for a walk. The Packingtons go to church. Rose sits down alone and ponders, but she is interrupted by Gilbert. As they talk, Rose confides in Gilbert; to him she can say that Walter is incapable of human love—that he loves only Svend and Anstey. After this confidential tête-à-tête, Gilbert goes for a walk, thinking about Rose and Walter. He conceives a plan: he goes to his brother and, after trapping Walter into admitting that he is guided by reason and not by emotions, Gilbert asks for Svend. He says that he and another surgeon are on the

brink of a tremendous scientific discovery, but they need a dog
for vivisection—not just *any* dog but an extraordinarily intelligent
and sensitive one.

Walter, who is, of course, greatly distressed, accuses his brother
of being cold and brutal, with no understanding of love and
loyalty. Gilbert counters by turning these words back upon
Walter himself; in the courts of law, he has been cold and
ruthless, logical but inhuman. Walter is in torment—but Gilbert
gives him no quarter. Finally, Walter has to admit his love for
this dog, but he still refuses the request. Gilbert, however, has
one more card to play: he tells his brother that the dog will
go blind within six months and therefore what little life is left
him might just as well be spent in advancing scientific knowledge. At this Walter gives in and surrenders the dog to his
brother. The whole business is, of course, a hoax that Gilbert
has conceived for the "good" of his brother and Rose. He knows
that he has to hurt his brother, to make him suffer, in order to
make him realize the power of love.

The next morning Walter wakens to the agony of a day without Svend. In defiance and alone, he pretends to be gay; and
he is charming to his guests. Rose does not understand what has
happened; she only knows that inside her husband has been
deeply wounded. Finally, she realizes that there is only one
explanation—something dreadful has happened to Svend. As
the day progresses toward evening, Walter wishes that the
people would go away; now he wants only Rose—Rose who can
be relied upon to understand and not increase his torment.
Finally he tells Rose—and she declares her love for him, tries
to reach out to comfort him; but he draws back; for he is not
yet ready for love. Asking her to account to their guests for
Svend's absence, he dismisses his wife.

On this day Anstey is open to a public that pours in to see
the gardens and the stately old manor house—to admire, in
short, the fortunate owners of so beautiful an estate. That
evening Gilbert telephones Walter to say that the operation is
over—that Svend is dead.

Rose looks for Walter to come to her bedroom that night,
but she is disappointed. She lies awake, waiting for him. At
about one in the morning, she smells smoke: Anstey is on fire.
In a high wind, the fire in the hearth has flared and the flames

have caught the curtains flying at the windows. Rose and Walter succeed in awakening everyone and in evacuating the house; but Anstey itself lies in ruins. The company assembles in the only part of the building saved—the servant's quarters in the rear, where they are Summers's guests. When Walter and Robin try to salvage some furniture and properties from the ruins, nothing can be found but a Wedgwood urn.

At length the company departs. Rose and Walter are alone. The only two passions of his life have been taken from him; but, in adversity, Walter has found strength—and love. With Rose, he plans a new life; they will live in the lodge and work the garden—just the two of them. The book ends when Gilbert, having heard over the wireless the news of the destruction of Anstey, returns Svend, safe and unharmed, to Rose, and confesses to her his purpose.

Sentimental as the plot sounds in a synopsis, the story is told simply, with flashes of humor that help to relieve the melodramatic taint. The reactions of the characters are realistic, and the portrait of Lady Juliet Quarles is especially good. A left-over from the Edwardian period, she is treated with the right admixture of satire and sympathy that makes Sackville-West's characterizations in the Edwardian novels memorable. And there are the usual bits of description of the gardens and of the house—descriptions of the English country-life which we have come to expect from a Sackville-West novel. Even the description of the dog reminds one of a sympathetic but semi-satiric essay she wrote on the resemblance of dogs to people, poking gentle fun at the English sportsman. The touch of mysticism (the visitation in the grotto of the satyr) also is typical of Sackville-West's concern with the mysteries of life, especially in the late novels; it also reminds one of E. M. Forster's little bits of whimsy, such as "The Celestial Omnibus."

IV No Signposts in the Sea

Sackville-West's last novel, *No Signposts in the Sea*, was published in 1961, the year before her death. Its plot may be stated briefly: the writer (the "I") is Edmund Carr, well-known journalist and authority on international affairs, who, learning that he has only a few months to live, takes a world cruise because the woman he loves will be a fellow passenger. Although he can never declare his love for this woman, a middle-aged widow named Laura Drysdale, he can at least speak with her, be near her, watch her. Laura gives Edmund a diary, and the story is told by means of this age-old device—we read his entries in the diary.

This little book is a gem, polished and cut with precision; technically, it is by far the best of the late novels. Every word seems weighed and counted. The diary technique is exceptionally well done; it obscures neither the plot nor the characterizations. The novelist herself, like her chief character, seems to have attained a heightened awareness of the preciosity of every moment, an appreciation of the small and simple pleasures.

The story opens with the speaker, the "I," describing some of his fellow passengers, who are typical travelers. For example, "there is the lonely questing English woman whom I instantly recognized as a menace. . . . Not bad-looking, and carefully made-up, she disguises the poverty of her mind and no doubt the starvation of her heart by a bright, eager manner, as an indifferent poet will seek to add interest to his lines by laying them out in the shape of a wine-glass, or an indifferent pastry-cook decorate his cakes with pink sugar roses."[12] Another passenger, Colonel Dalrymple, is also a typical English character; and Sackville-West draws him with gentle satire. A conformist, he expresses the expected conservative ideas of an English aristocrat; yet he is intelligent, chivalrous towards women in an old-fashioned way, well-informed, and well-travelled. With the writer, he and Laura make a trio; and, after a time, Edmund Carr finds himself growing jealous of the colonel, whom he considers a rival.

Edmund and Laura spend much time together but simply as friends. They go ashore on trips, they spend a night together in a villa, they share the same delights and find pleasure in a sunset and in a thunderstorm at sea. When they finally talk about marriage, Laura tells Edmund that she was married to Tommy Drysdale, who was killed in the war; but she confesses that the marriage was not successful—at least, not for her. It is Edmund's first knowledge that this union was not a happy one. Laura's concept of marriage sounds much like the author's, for Laura declares her love of independence, her need for equality in marriage: "I cannot abide the Mr. and Mrs. Noah attitude towards marriage,"[13] she says. When Edmund asks her for a recipe for a workable marriage, her reply is that such a marriage must be based upon mutual respect and upon the same set of values; husband and wife must avoid hurting each other; they should have separate bedrooms (and sitting-rooms, too, if possible). Surely Sackville-West and Harold Nicolson's marriage was founded upon "the same set of values"—the most essential element in the recipe.

At the end of the conversation, Laura admits that she is in love. Edmund, in his complete naïveté, thinks the object of her love is Dalrymple; but, when he mentions the colonel's name, Laura calls him a fool and runs off. That evening, while recording this conversation in his diary, Edmund begins to realize the truth—Laura has fallen in love with him. But, even as the thought dawns and he starts to write it down, he dies of a heart attack.

The reader finishes this last book by Sackville-West with a sigh of regret that there is not another one. Yet he is glad that there was no diminishing of power here; he is grateful for the technical excellence of this novel in all its aspects. Especially satisfying is the "plain" style of writing; the story is told without sentimentality, with great economy of expression. And the reader feels, through the characterizations and the ideas expressed, that he has reached deep into the personality of the author herself.

V *Conclusion*

These four late novels appear, on the surface, to have little in common. *Grand Canyon* is a war novel; *The Devil at Westease*, a mystery; *The Easter Party*, a bit of English whimsy; and *No Signposts in the Sea*, a love story. But, although they differ in theme and thesis, they present what we have come to recognize as typical Sackville-West ideas. *Grand Canyon* contains a metaphysical concept of the power of love (a concept we found in *Grey Wethers* and in *The Eagle and the Dove*); *The Devil at Westease* treats again the duality of good and evil in man, the "heart of darkness" theme; *The Easter Party* utilizes once again V. Sackville-West's love of Knole and English tradition; *No Signposts in the Sea* is concerned with the "aloneness of us all," the difficulty—even the impossibility—of communication between two people.

But, if we except *Grand Canyon,* which is written in Miss Sackville-West's florid style, we discover that stylistically and technically the other three novels are cut from the same cloth. All three are short, terse novelettes; there is an increasing economy in expression, there are fewer characters, and the plot structure is very simple. These qualities are those generally to be expected as an artist matures. it is a cliché that simplicity in any art marks a high state of sophistication and achievement, for it is most difficult to attain. Even the diary technique of *No Signposts in the Sea,* which in the hands of a less skilled craftsman often leads to verbosity, does not impede the swift flow of thought; and V. Sackville-West in these late novels learned to rein in her delight in description. The beauty of Anstey in *The Easter Party,* the tranquility of the village Westease, and the moods of the sea in *No Signposts in the Sea* are sketched lightly here and there throughout the novel; but we never feel overwhelmed by lengthy nature descriptions. These novels are not "profound," not noteworthy for their originality; but they are entertaining and rewarding for those who enjoy a good story sensitively and simply told.

CHAPTER 10

Appraisals

> "Everyone thinks himself able to review fiction."
> V. Sackville-West[1]

I *Critics: English and American*

NO extensive critical or scholarly studies have been made of
Sackville-West's work; all that there are are a few short
sketches and, of course, the reviews of her books as they were
released.[2] In reading the appraisals of the critics, I note two
facts: one, that favorable or unfavorable reviews may be found
for almost every one of her books; second, that the British press
was not more laudatory than the American—in fact, if anything,
the American reviews are more enthusiastic. Indeed, Sackville-
West achieved her first literary success in the United States.

If there is any critical distinction to be made on the basis
of national appeal, it must concern her poetry. Since her two long
poems, *The Land* and *The Garden,* deal with the English countryside, it is not surprising that these works communicate more
readily and perceptively to her countrymen. For example, the
review of *The Land* in the London *Times* stressed the author's
deep emotional attachment to the country: "In refusing reso-
lutely to sentimentalize the labourer's life she tends to over-
emphasize its dourness and austerity. Yet her poem, like the
land itself, is full of the bounty that is the reward of toil and the
beauty that blooms in a world of fact mastered by patient
cultivation. Whether she writes of the choice of day for spring-
sowing, of bee-keeping, rick-building or thatching, of sheep-
shearing, ploughing or wood-craft, she draws upon sound rural
erudition."[3]

But we Americans are likely to find the subject not weighty
enough for the form and style—partly, no doubt, because we
have lost the feeling of closeness to nature; we no longer under-

stand the spirit of an agrarian society and the eclogue is, for us, an archaic poetic form. We are inclined, therefore, to agree with Conrad Aiken (who is, however, an anglophile) that "Miss Sackville-West is a little too deliberate in her attack, a little too self-conscious in her immersion in the landscape. She is inclined to overwhelm us with detail."[4] Yet, in spite of the Romantic tone and the remoteness of the subject-matter, we admire the polish, the graceful rhythms—in sum, the poetic essence of her poetry when at its best.

Concerning Miss Sackville-West as a biographer, the critics generally applauded *Pepita* as highly successful because of its vitality, high color, and gusto. The London *Times* review gave it unstinted praise: "This delightful book is divided into two parts: both are fascinating, the first for a true, though complicated, narrative which, if invented by a novelist, would be deemed incredible; and the second for its lifelike picture of a woman of whom Rudyard Kipling wrote: 'on mature reflection, the most wonderful person I have ever met.' "[5] And L. A. Strong, in the *Spectator,* was most enthusiastic: "it is the second part which, for me at any rate, makes the book. In it Miss Sackville-West's cool, half humorous detachment gives way to something no less humorless, no less controlled, but warmer, richer, and quite beautiful. I have always been an admirer of Miss Sackville-West's writing, but in these last chapters she has surpassed herself. Even *All Passion Spent* can hardly match them. Affection has lit and shot her prose with new colours. The balance is as perfect as the taste."[6]

As for her other works of biography and history, the critics find her accurate and sound in scholarship but rather uninspired in bringing her characters to life. A. A. Pursell, however, declared *Saint Joan of Arc* to be not only objective in its treatment and thorough in scholarship but also artistically satisfying in its building up of climaxes and in its dramatic power.[7] For Geoffrey Bruun, in the *Yale Review,* the author's honesty in admitting that she has no explanation for Joan's voices and other mystic manifestations resulted in an ambiguous and confusing point of view; but he found the book, on the whole, entertaining.[8] Most of the critics concur in declaring this biography one of Miss Sackville-West's finest. About the rest of her work in this genre, the critics were less enthusiastic.

But we should turn to the appraisals of Miss Sackville-West's best-known works, her novels. Again the critical reviews present opposing estimates. Hugh Walpole ranked Miss Sackville-West with Virginia Woolf and Rebecca West.[9] Most reviewers of *All Passion Spent* noted the originality of its structure and style, and commented upon the beautiful artistry in the creation of mood and in the delicacy of the thematic treatment. For example, W. E. Harris of the Boston *Transcript* wrote: "Ordinary plotting is thrown nimbly aside.... Nothing comes obviously from its conservative, routine source. Yet out of the chaos Miss Sackville-West has wrought order, simplicity... over all is folded a tapestry of beautiful writing."[10]

In spite of the popular success of *The Edwardians*, the reviews were not uncritical. Clifton Fadiman, writing in *The Nation*, felt that the satire did not quite succeed because the author was at least partly in sympathy with the Edwardian world she was ridiculing: "To judge from the elaborate literary apparatus Miss Sackville-West employs, one supposes that she intended a scandalously bitter satire.... But she lacks either the skill or the courage to do more than poke a little fun...."[11] On the other hand, Louis Kronenberger found the satire pointed, even brilliant: "It comes close to being distinguished and even closer to being witty; it will bear comparison, though it cannot quite sustain it, with the very finest novels of manners."[12] Fanny Butcher, in the Chicago *Daily Tribune*, went even further to call it "A perfect novel of manners, plus a certain keen and brilliant satire."[13]

In judging the last of the Edwardian novels, *Family History*, the London *Times* found it "common-place," largely because it follows the structure of the orthodox novel.[14] Dorothea Brande, however, believed the characters to be vividly portrayed and the situations well handled; still, she saw the book as "largely entertainment."[15]

Finally, we should glance at reviews of Miss Sackville-West's late novels. Most critics dismissed *The Devil at Westease* and *The Easter Party* as minor works, as not equal to the standard of the Edwardian novels. To be sure, the books are really novelettes, and are not to be taken too seriously; the author herself must have so regarded them. For Edward Wagenknecht, Walter did not "come alive" because the author had not explored deeply enough the psychological problem she posed.[16] But, if Wagenknecht found *The Easter Party* superficial in its psychological characterization, Aileen Pippett declared V. Sackville-West's last novel, *No Signposts in the Sea*, to be a profound study of human nature and of the basic emotions: "There is more in this short novel than in many twice its length, but not more than could be expected of this author. A deceptively simple style, supple, elegant, and firm, shows the discipline of the poet.... This is, above all, a love story...the richness of texture and depth of feeling show this to be the work of a mature mind and a skilled artist, worthy to rank with the best she has ever written."[17] It is fitting and most satisfying to close this survey of criticism with Miss Pippett's comment, for it successfully summarizes the accomplishments of V. Sackville-West.

II *Conclusion*

From these samplings of reviews, three main criticisms emerge: Miss Sackville-West's handling of mood and of setting is better than her characterizations; her matter is often "thin"; she sometimes seems reluctant to expose in depth an idea or the inner reality of a character. Since it was Hugh Walpole's opinion that Sackville-West was more skillful in creating atmosphere than character,[18] we may credit much of this criticism to his influence. But we should note that he made his comment in 1930 before *All Passion Spent* had been published; and we would have to agree that in *Heritage, Grey Wethers, Challenge,* and *The Edwardians* descriptions of setting and mood outweigh, generally speaking, the characterizations. The poet sometimes triumphed over the novelist. But, as Sackville-West matured in her art, she achieved a nice balance between these two aspects. She created some unforgettable characters; and among them are Lady Slane in *All Passion Spent*, Kato in *Challenge*, Evelyn Jarrold in *Family History*, Silas Dene in *The Dragon in Shallow Waters*, and Shirin Wilson in *The Dark Island*.

The charges that the plot and ideas that Sackville-West employed are weak and fragile and that she was reluctant to explore in depth a problem or concept seem to stem from a misunderstanding of her purpose and method. First of all, the impression of fragility often results from her desire to be concerned with the evanescent and intangible emotions of which she was always aware. As we learn from her letters, she painstakingly worked to communicate an emotion created by a sudden recall of the past or by an interplay of personalities.[19] To accomplish this effect, she would sacrifice plot, even character credibility. And another facet of Sackville-West's art is also important: she was always conscious of the essential uniqueness and mystery of each individual, actual or fictional. For this reason—especially in those novels exploring the "heart of darkness" theme—she did not push her character analyses to the ultimate; she hesitated to turn the sword in the wound. Herein lies perchance an English trait: a horror of invading a human being's privacy—even if this creature is a figment of the imagination. A strong part of Sackville-West's philosophy was a kind of hypersensitivity, a belief that the human mystery must be respected; in fact, that it cannot be fully grasped by another—perhaps not even by the person himself.

But even more important in this regard was her artistic creed: the reader is an active part of the story and must bring an alert, sensitive imagination to a work of art in order to read between the lines. As with E. M. Forster's novels, Sackville-West's must be read in this fashion. Very rarely did she belabor a point or deal violently with her plot: *Grand Canyon* and *The Dragon in Shallow Waters* are the only two exceptions that come to mind.

After reading through Miss Sackville-West's works, we cannot help feeling that we have come close to knowing—as close, perhaps, as we ever come—a fine artist. Much of herself went into her writing, which is often autobiographical and highly subjective. For example, she generally expressed her personal views and convictions candidly, without affectation—as she did in the passage quoted from *Joan of Arc* in which Sackville-West so clearly summarized her own religious convictions.

Any prediction about which of her works will live is hazardous, but the Edwardian novels, *Challenge* and *No Signposts in the Sea* will survive for some time to come as outstanding examples of twentieth-century fiction; *Pepita* will rank among the finest, most readable biographies; and some of the short stories—"The Heir," "Thirty Clocks Strike the Hours," "The Death of Noble Godavary"—will find their way into standard anthologies of this genre. Of Sackville-West's poems, *The Land*

and some of her short lyrics deserve a place in the noble tradition of English poetry. If Victoria Sackville-West attained a position below the literary "greats," she nonetheless achieved a permanent niche in English literature and established her right to be recognized as one of the significant literary figures of the twentieth century.

Notes and References

Chapter One

1. *The Diaries and Letters of Sir Harold Nicolson*, ed. by Nigel Nicolson (New York, 1966), I, 158.
2. Roger Ascham, *The Scholemaster* (London, 1870), pp. 17-20.
3. V. Sackville-West, *Knole and The Sackvilles* (London, 1922), p. 122. This book is discussed in greater detail in chapter 3.
4. *Ibid.*, p. 115.
5. *Ibid.*, p. 156.
6. *Ibid.*, p. 218.
7. *Ibid.*, p. 219.
8. *Ibid.*, pp. 219-20.
9. V. Sackville-West, *Pepita* (New York, 1937), p. 240.
10. *Ibid.*, p. 242.
11. *The Diaries and Letters of Sir Harold Nicolson*, I, 19.
12. *Pepita*, p. 243.
13. *Ibid.*, p. 244.
14. *The Diaries and Letters of Sir Harold Nicolson*, I, 20.
15. *Ibid.*, I, 20.
16. *Ibid.*, I, 21.
17. *Ibid.*, I, 21.
18. *Ibid.*, II, 57.
19. *Ibid.*, I, 92
20. *Ibid.*, I, 33-4.
21. *Ibid.*, I, 158.
22. *Ibid.*, I, 349.
23. *Ibid.*, I, 129-30.
24. *Ibid.*, I, 135-36.
25. *Ibid.*, I, 175.
26. *Ibid.*, I, 301-2.
27. *Ibid.*, I, 311.
28. *Ibid.*, I, 368.
29. *Ibid.*, I, 379.
30. *Ibid.*, I, 379.
31. *Ibid.*, I, 404-5.
32. John Milton, "Samson Agonistes," *Complete English Poetry of John Milton*, ed. by John Shawcross (New York, 1963), p. 195, ll. 1745-57.

Chapter Two

1. *The Diaries and Letters of Sir Harold Nicolson,* I, 18.
2. *Ibid.,* II, 110.
3. Aileen Pippett, *The Moth and the Star: A Biography of Virginia Woolf* (Boston, 1953), p. 58.
4. J. K. Johnstone, *The Bloomsbury Group* (New York), pp. 60-2.
5. *Ibid.,* p. 61.
6. See chapter 3, where I discuss V. Sackville-West's *Joan of Arc.*
7. *The Diaries and Letters of Sir Harold Nicolson,* I, 350-51.
8. Pippett, p. 74.
9. Jean Guiguet, *Virginia Woolf and Her Works* (New York, 1965), p. 278.
10. *The Diaries and Letters of Sir Harold Nicolson,* I, 30.
11. Guiguet, p. 258.
12. *Ibid.,* p. 258.
13. Frank Baldanza, *"Orlando* and the Sackvilles," *Publications of the Modern Language Association,* LXX, I (March, 1955), 274.
14. Virginia Woolf, *Orlando: A Biography* (New York, 1928), p. 75.
15. *Ibid.,* p. 143.
16. *Ibid.,* p. 318.
17. Baldanza, 279n.
18. Virginia Woolf, *A Writer's Diary* (New York, 1953), p. 189.
19. *The Diaries and Letters of Sir Harold Nicolson,* I, 350.

Chapter Three

1. *The Diary of The Lady Anne Clifford* (New York, 1923), p. xxiv.
2. *Passenger to Teheran* (New York, 1927), p. 123.
3. *English Country Houses* (London, 1942), p. 13.
4. *Ibid.,* p. 7.
5. *Knole and the Sackvilles,* p. 2.
6. *Ibid.,* p. 144.
7. *Ibid.,* p. 149.
8. *Ibid.,* p. 151.
9. *Pepita,* p. 244.
10. *Ibid.,* p. 253.
11. *Ibid.,* p. 279.
12. V. Sackville-West, *Joan of Arc* (New York, 1936), p. 214.
13. *Ibid.,* p. 237.
14. *Ibid.,* pp. 344-45.
15. *The Diaries and Letters of Sir Harold Nicolson,* II, 333.
16. Quoted by V. Sackville-West, *The Eagle and the Dove: A Study in Contrasts* (New York, 1943), p. 8.

17. *Ibid.*, p. 109. This miracle Thérèse discusses in her auto-biography.

18. *Ibid.*, p. 117.

19. *Ibid.*, p. 123.

20. *Daughter of France* (New York, 1959), p. 199.

21. "George Eliot," *The Great Victorians,* ed. by H. J. Massingham and Hugh Massingham (New York, 1932), p. 173.

22. "Walter de la Mare and *The Traveler,*" *Proceedings of the British Academy of Arts and Sciences* (1939), p. 26.

Chapter Four

1. *The Diaries and Letters of Sir Harold Nicolson,* II, 420.

2. *Pepita,* p. 305.

3. Grant Overton, *Authors of the Day* (New York, 1923), p. 120.

4. Woolf, *A Writer's Diary,* p. 107. She wrote an amusing description of this event, the awarding of the Hawthornden Prize.

5. *The Diaries and Letters of Sir Harold Nicolson,* I, 420-21.

6. *The Land* (New York, 1927), p. 24.

7. *Ibid.*, p. 20.

8. *Ibid.*, p. 79.

9. *The Garden* (New York, 1946), p. 56.

10. *The Land,* pp. 82-3.

11. *The Garden,* p. 15.

12. *Ibid.*, p. 24.

13. *Ibid.*, p. 24.

14. *Ibid.*, p. 20.

15. *Ibid.*, p. 66.

16. *Ibid.*, p. 129.

17. *The Diaries and Letters of Sir Harold Nicolson,* II, 420.

18. *Collected Poems* (New York, 1943), pp. 111-14.

19. *Ibid.*, pp. 144-45.

20. *The Diaries and Letters of Sir Harold Nicolson,* II, 447-48.

21. *Ibid.*, II, 447-48.

22. *Ibid.*, p. 290.

23. *Ibid.*, III, 38. This is an interesting letter to her husband concerning her poetry.

Chapter Five

1. E. L. Broun, *New York Times* (June 12, 1932), p. 7.

2. Stuart Petrie Brodie Mais, *Some Modern Authors* (New York, 1923), p. 144.

3. *Thirty Clocks Strike the Hour and Other Stories* (New York, 1929), pp. 229-30.

4. *Ibid.*, p. 280.

Chapter Six

1. *Heritage* (New York, 1919), p. 16.
2. *Ibid.*, pp. 16-17.
3. *Ibid.*, p. 316.
4. *Ibid.*, p. 317.
5. Katherine Mansfield, *Novels and Novelists* (Boston, 1930), p. 29.
6. *Heritage*, pp. 13-14.
7. *The Dragon in Shallow Waters* (New York, 1922), p. 162.
8. *Ibid.*, p. 257.
9. *Ibid.*, p. 263.
10. *Ibid.*, p. 281.
11. *Grey Wethers* (New York, 1923), p. 43.
12. *Ibid.*, p. 224.
13. *Ibid.*, p. 260.
14. *Ibid.*, p. 230.
15. *Ibid.*, p. 300.
16. *Heritage*, pp. 36-7.
17. Elizabeth A. Drew, *The Modern Novel* (New York, 1926), p. 126.
18. *Grey Wethers*, p. 224.
19. Woolf, *A Writer's Diary*, p. 118.

Chapter Seven

1. *Challenge* (New York, 1923), p. 172.
2. *Ibid.*, p. 172.
3. *Ibid.*, p. 83.
4. *Ibid.*, p. 291.
5. *Ibid.*, p. 42.
6. *Ibid.*, p. 65.
7. *Ibid.*, p. 62.
8. Drew, p. 245.
9. *Seducers in Ecuador* (New York, 1925), p. 16.
10. *The Dark Island* (New York, 1934), pp. 42-43.

Chapter Eight

1. *The Diaries and Letters of Sir Harold Nicolson*, I, 23.
2. *Ibid.*, I, 69.
3. *All Passion Spent* (New York, 1931), p. 129.
4. *Ibid.*, p. 262.
5. *Ibid.*, p. 127.
6. *Ibid.*, p. 194.

7. *Ibid.*, p. 113.
8. *Ibid.*, p. 109.
9. *The Edwardians* (New York, 1930), p. 11.
10. *Ibid.*, p. 272.
11. *Ibid.*, p. 272.
12. *Ibid.*, pp. 12-14.
13. *Ibid.*, p. 237.
14. *Ibid.*, p. 219.
15. *Ibid.*, p. 219.
16. *Ibid.*, p. 58.
17. *The Diaries and Letters of Sir Harold Nicolson*, I, 119.
18. V. Sackville-West, *Family History* (New York, 1932), pp. 39-40.
19. *Ibid.*, p. 170.
20. *Ibid.*, p. 23.
21. *Ibid.*, p. 58.
22. *Ibid.*, p. 65.
23. *Ibid.*, p. 104.
24. *Ibid.*, pp. 120-21.
25. Clifton Fadiman, *Nation*, XV (October, 1930), 413.
26. W. E. Harris, *Boston Transcript* (September 5, 1931), 8.
27. Dorothea Brande, *Bookman*, LXXV (November 1932), 734.

Chapter Nine

1. *The Diaries and Letters of Sir Harold Nicolson*, II, 420.
2. *Ibid.*, I, 135-36 (See also Chapter 1, pp. 27-28).
3. *The Grand Canyon* (New York, 1942), p. 47.
4. *Ibid.*, pp. 81-83.
5. *Ibid.*, p. 229.
6. *Ibid.*, p. 202.
7. *Ibid.*, pp. 302-3.
8. *Ibid.*, p. 303.
9. *Ibid.*, p. 285.
10. *Ibid.*, p. 275.
11. *The Devil at Westease* (New York, 1946), pp. 218-19.
12. V. Sackville-West, *No Signposts in the Sea* (New York, 1953), p. 13. We are reminded that Miles Vane-Merrick in *Family History* used the same metaphor concerning marriage (See Chapter 8, p. 118).
13. *Ibid.*, p. 82.

Chapter Ten

1. "Literary Criticism Hit," *New York Times* (January 12, 1933), 15.

2. I must acknowledge an excellent unpublished Columbia University master's thesis, just come to my attention, which deals with V. Sackville-West's four novels of the 1930's. Its author is Nancy M. MacKnight, who is now expanding this thesis into a doctoral dissertation.

3. (London) *Times Literary Supplement* (October 21, 1926), 716.

4. *The Independent*, CXVIII (February 26, 1927), 246.

5. (London) *Times Literary Supplement* (October 30, 1937), 796.

6. *The Spectator*, CLVIX (November 19, 1937), 159.

7. *America*, LVI (October 7, 1936), 46.

8. *Yale Review*, XXVI (Winter, 1937), 398.

9. Hugh Walpole, "V. Sackville-West," *Bookman*, LXXII (September, 1930), 21-26.

10. *Boston Transcript* (September 5, 1931), 8.

11. *The Nation*, CXXXI (October 13, 1930), 413.

12. *The New York Times* (September 7, 1930), 7.

13. *Chicago Daily Tribune* (September 13, 1930), 9.

14. (London) *Times Literary Supplement* (October 13, 1933), 730.

15. *Bookman*, LXXV (November, 1932), 734.

16. *Chicago Sunday Tribune* (February 15, 1953), 3.

17. *The Saturday Review*, XLIV (April 22, 1961), 24.

18. See note 9, Chapter 10.

19. There are a number of places in *The Diaries and Letters of Sir Harold Nicolson* when V. Sackville-West speaks of her problems of writing. It was not for her an easy task. (See II, 269; II, 434-35; II, 447-48; III, 297; III, 346-47.)

Selected Bibliography

PRIMARY SOURCES

This bibliography of V. Sackville-West's writings is an inclusive one; but I indicate the major works by an asterisk. I have also listed as primary source material the three volumes of *The Diaries and Letters of Sir Harold Nicolson,* edited by Nigel Nicolson, because this work includes excerpts from an unfinished autobiography of V. Sackville-West and her letters to her husband.

Almost all of V. Sackville-West's books were first published in England and then in the United States; I, however, have listed the edition I used for this study.

Extremely useful is a "Selected List of Writings by and About V. Sackville-West" by Florence Boochevre, published in *The Bulletin of Bibliography,* 16, 1 (1938), 113-15.

All Passion Spent. Garden City: Doubleday, Doran and Co., 1931.
Andrew Marvell. London: Faber and Faber, 1929.
Another World than This. London: M. Joseph, 1945. Anthology of poetry compiled by V. Sackville-West and Sir Harold Nicolson.
Aphra Behn, the Incomparable Astrea. London: G. Howe, Ltd., 1927.
et al. Beginnings. London: Nelson and Son, 1935.
Challenge. New York: G. H. Doran and Co., 1923.
Collected Poems. Garden City: Doubleday, Doran and Co., 1934.
"The Comet." In (London) *Times Literary Supplement* (April 17, 1943), 198.
Country Notes. New York: Harper and Sons, 1940.
Country Notes in Wartime. Garden City: Doubleday, Doran and Co., 1941.
The Dark Island. Garden City: Doubleday, Doran and Co., 1936.
Daughter of France: the Life of Anne Marie Louise d'Orleans (1627-1693). Garden City: Doubleday and Co., 1959.
The Devil at Westease. Garden City: Doubleday and Co., 1946.
The Diaries and Letters of Sir Harold Nicolson. Nigel Nicolson, ed. 3 vols. New York: Atheneum, 1966-67.
The Diary of Lady Anne Clifford. New York: George H. Doran and Co., 1923. Ed. by V. Sackville-West, with introduction.
The Dragon in Shallow Waters. New York: Putnam, 1922.

151

The Eagle and the Dove, A Study in Contrasts. Garden City: Doubleday, Doran and Co., 1944.

The Easter Party. Garden City: Doubleday and Co., 1953.

The Edwardians. Garden City: Doubleday, Doran and Co., 1930.

Sackville-West, V. and Edward. *Elegies from the Castle of Duino* by Rainer Maria Rilke. Translated from the German. London: Hogarth Press, 1931.

English Country Houses. London: W. Collins, 1942.

Even More for Your Garden. London: M. Joseph, 1958. Collection of articles published in *The Observer* from April 8, 1955 to October 6, 1957.

Faces: Profiles of Dogs. London: Harvill Press, 1961.

"Falling in Love." In *Essays of the Year 1933-1934.* London: Argonaut, 1934.

Family History. Garden City: Doubleday, Doran and Co., 1932.

"Les Français parlent aux Français" (Poem). In (London) *Times Literary Supplement* (July 15, 1944), 340.

"The Future of the Novel." In *Bookman,* LXXII (December, 1930), 350-51.

The Garden. Garden City: Doubleday and Co., 1946.

"George Eliot." In *The Great Victorians.* Ed. by H. J. Massingham and Hugh Massingham. Garden City: Doubleday, Doran and Co., 1932.

Grand Canyon. Garden City: Doubleday, Doran and Co., 1942.

Grey Wethers: A Romantic Novel. New York: George H. Doran Co., 1923.

The Heir: A Love Story. George H. Doran Co., 1922. A collection of short stories.

Heritage. New York: George H. Doran Co., 1919.

et al. *How Does Your Garden Grow?* London: Allen and Unwin, 1935.

"Impressions of a Traveller." In (London) *Times* (January 5, 1931), p. 16.

"In the Highlands of the French Savoy." In *Travel,* LVI (May, 1930), p. 18.

In Your Garden. London: M. Joseph, 1951.

In Your Garden Again. London: M. Joseph, 1953.

Invitation to Cast Out Care. London: Faber and Faber, 1931. Also in *Collected Poems.*

A *Joy of Gardening.* New York: Harper and Sons, 1958. Ed. by Hermine Popper.

The King's Daughter. London: Hogarth Press, 1929. Also in *Collected Poems.*

Knole and the Sackvilles. New York: George H. Doran Co., 1922.

°The Land. New York: George H. Doran Co., 1927. Also in *Collected Poems.*

"Memory—Bad and Good," *Spectator,* LIV (July 30, 1932), 148-49.

More for Your Garden. London: M. Joseph, 1955.

°No Signposts in the Sea. Garden City: Doubleday and Co., 1961.

Nursery Rhymes. London: Drohmore Press, 1947.

Orchard and Vineyard. London: Lane, Bodley Head, 1921.

"Our Future Beckons," *Pictorial Review* (November, 1933), pp. 19+.

"Outdoor Life." *The Character of England.* Oxford: Oxford University Press, 1947.

°Passenger to Teheran. New York: George H. Doran Co., 1927.

°Pepita. Garden City: Doubleday, Doran and Co., 1937.

Poems of West and East. London: J. Lane, 1918.

Introduction to *Prose and Poetry,* by Alice C. Meynell. London: J. Cape, 1947.

°Saint Joan of Arc. Garden City: Doubleday, Doran and Co., 1936.

"Searchlights," (London) *Times Literary Supplement* (September 16, 1944), p. 447.

°Seducers in Ecuador. New York: George H. Doran Co., 1925.

°Selected Poems. London: Hogarth Press, 1941.

Some Flowers. London: Cobden-Sanderson, 1937.

"Some Tendencies of Modern English Poetry," *Royal Society of Literature of the United Kingdom,* VII (1927), 39-54.

"Steeped in the Courtesy of More Leisurely Centuries," *Arts and Decoration* (December, 1936), pp. 20-23. An article about Knole.

"The Stone Manger." (London) *Times Literary Supplement* (December 23, 1944), p. 620.

"Street Music." *Essays of the Year 1931-1932.* London, Argonaut, 1932.

°Thirty Clocks Strike the Hour and Other Stories. Garden City: Doubleday, Doran and Co., 1932.

°Twelve Days: An Account of A Journey Across the Bakhtari Mountains in Southwestern Persia. New York: Doubleday, Doran and Co., 1928.

"Walter de la Mare and the Traveler." In *Proceedings of the British Academy,* XXXIX (1953), 23-26.

"Women Poets of the 'Seventies." In *Royal Society of Literature of the United Kingdom,* IX (1929), 111-32.

The Women's Land Army. London: M. Joseph, 1944.

SECONDARY SOURCES

A. Articles about V. Sackville-West

> (There are surprisingly few significant articles about
> V. Sackville-West, for she has been unduly neglected
> by scholars.)

BALDANZA, FRANK. "Orlando and the Sackvilles," *Publications of
the Modern Language Association*. LXX, 1 (March, 1955),
274-79. This article was the first to point out the parallels
between Orlando and V. Sackville-West.

CHESSON, W. H. "V. Sackville-West," *Bookman*, LXV (February,
1924), 243-44. An early appraisal of V. Sackville-West.

CHURCH, RICHARD. *Eight for Immortality*. London: Dent and Co.,
1941. Contains a fine biographical sketch of V. Sackville-West.

JACKSON, KATHERINE GAUSS. "Gets What She Wants," *Scribner's*
(November, 1936), 84. Presents a sketch of V. Sackville-West,
the woman.

"Literary Criticism Hit," *New York Times* (January 12, 1933), p. 15.
Report of a lecture given by V. Sackville-West at Yale.

"Married Authors Clash on Careers," *New York Times* (January 10,
1933), p. 3. Report of a debate between the Nicolsons, given
at the Brooklyn Academy of Music.

WALPOLE, HUGH. "V Sackville-West," *Bookman*, LXXII (September,
1930), 21-26. Perceptive evaluation of the prose style of V.
Sackville-West.

WILL, J. S. "The New Writers, 21," *Canadian Forum*, XI (September, 1931), 462-63. Presents evaluations of specific works of
V. Sackville-West.

B. Reviews of books by V. Sackville-West

> Below are listed only a few of the significant reviews
> of Miss Sackville-West's best known works. These re-
> views present a sampling of the opinions of both English
> and American critics. References to other reviews are
> to be found in the text and are documented in the
> footnotes. (See Chapter 10.)

1. *All Passion Spent.*
   HARRIS, W. E. *Boston Transcript* (September 5, 1931), p. 8. A
   fine appreciation of the originality of this work.
   STRONG, L. A. G. *Spectator*, CXLVI (May 30, 1931), 872. Tribute
   to V. Sackville-West as a stylist.

2. *The Easter Party.*

WAGENKNECHT, EDWARD. *Chicago Sunday Tribune* (February 15, 1953), p. 3. "For a new writer this novel would be rated a brilliant performance. From one of Miss Sackville-West's achievement it seems puzzling and more than a little disappointing." The major criticism is a lack of depth in the interpretation of Walter's character.

3. *The Edwardians.*

BUTCHER, FANNY. *Chicago Daily Tribune* (September 13, 1930), p. 9. "A perfect novel of manners, plus a certain keen and brilliant satire."

FADIMAN, CLIFTON P. *Nation*, CXXXI (October 15, 1930), 413. One of the most devastating reviews of this book.

KRONENBERGER, LOUIS. *The New York Times* (September 7, 1930), p. 7. Highly laudatory review; ranks the novel "among the very finest novels of manners."

4. *Family History.*

BRANDE, DOROTHEA. *Bookman*, LXXV (November, 1932), 734. Thoughtful estimate of the strong and weak points of the novel.

(London) *Times Literary Supplement* (October 13, 1932), p. 730. Criticism of the employment of the traditional novel form. "It would probably be impossible for Miss Sackville-West to write an uninteresting book, but she is at her best only when she avoids the common road."

5. *Joan of Arc.*

BRUUN, GEOFFREY. *Yale Review*, XXVI (Winter, 1937), 398. Sympathetic criticism of V. Sackville-West as a biographer: comments on the sincerity and thoroughness of the work. However, this critic finds confusing the fact that V. Sackville-West does not resolve the problem of Joan's "voices."

PURSELL, A. A. *America*, LVI (October 7, 1936), 46. Commends especially the scholarship and style.

6. *The Land.*

AIKEN, CONRAD. *The Independent*, CXVIII (February 26, 1927), 246. Appreciation of the poem as a whole, but finds it a little precious and too heavily laden with detail.

Boston Transcript (October 29, 1927), p. 8. "A poetic saga of the land and the beauties of the changing seasons."

7. *No Signposts in the Sea.*

PIPPETT, AILEEN. *The Saturday Review*, XLIV (April 22, 1961), 24. "The richness of texture and depth of feeling show this to be the work of a mature mind and a skilled artist."

8. *Pepita.*

STRONG, L. A. G. *The Spectator,* CLIX, Sup. 24 (November 19, 1937), 59. Excellent appraisal of Miss Sackville-West's style and ability to organize her material.

(London) *Times Literary Supplement* (October 30, 1937), p. 796. A laudatory review, praising Miss Sackville-West for creating "a life-like picture of a woman."

9. *Thirty Clocks Strike the Hour and Other Stories.*

BROWN, E. L. *The New York Times* (June 12, 1932), p. 71. An appreciation of V. Sackville-West's short stories as a collection "of great distinction."

Saturday Review of Literature, VIII (June 25, 1932), 803. "These stories are all exquisite, and nearly all a little thin and fragile."

C. Other Secondary Sources

DREW, ELIZABETH A. *The Modern Novel.* New York: Harcourt, Brace and Co., 1926. Interesting comments on V. Sackville-West's early novels.

GUIGUET, JEAN. *Virginia Woolf and Her Works.* Translated by Jean Stewart. New York: Harcourt, Brace and World, Inc., 1965. Useful work for a discussion of *Orlando* and the friendship of V. Woolf and V. Sackville-West.

JOHNSTONE, J. K. *The Bloomsbury Group.* New York: The Noonday Press, 1954. Presents the history and the significant ideas of the group.

KUNITZ, STANLEY J. *Twentieth Century Authors.* New York: The Wilson Co., 1955. Brief life of V. Sackville-West.

MAIS, STUART PETRE BRODIE. *Some Modern Authors.* London: Richards, 1923. Contains a brief analysis of V. Sackville-West's early style.

MANSFIELD, KATHERINE. *Novels and Novelists.* Boston: Beacon Press, 1930. Discusses *Heritage.*

MARBLE, ANNIE RUSSELL. *A Study of the Modern Novel: British and American, Since 1900.* New York: D. Appleton and Co., 1928. Contains a brief critical estimate of V. Sackville-West's early novels.

MOORE, GEORGE EDWARD. *Principia Ethica.* Cambridge: Cambridge University Press, 1959. Statement of the esthetic principles that influenced the Bloomsbury Group.

NEWBOLT, HENRY JOHN. *New Paths on Helicon.* London: Nelson, 1927. Mentions briefly V. Sackville-West's poetry.

OVERTON, GRANT. "The Lady of a Tradition—Miss Sackville-West." *American Nights Entertainment.* New York: Appleton and Co.,

1923. Discusses the influence of Knole and of the childhood environment upon V. Sackville-West's writings.

PHILLIP, CHARLES J. B. *The History of the Sackville Family*. London: Cassell, 1930. Useful for family background.

PIPPETT, AILEEN. *The Moth and the Star: A Biography of Virginia Woolf*. Boston: Little, Brown and Co., 1953. Thorough study of V. Woolf; quotes excerpts from the unpublished correspondence between V. Woolf and V. Sackville-West. Presents a lucid explanation of the aims and ideals of the Bloomsbury Group.

UNTERMEYER, LOUIS. *Modern British Poetry*. New York: Harcourt, Brace and Co., 1930. Has a brief biography; some criticism of V. Sackville-West's work (particularly *The Land*) and its significance.

WOOLF, VIRGINIA. *The Death of the Moth*. New York: Harcourt, Brace and Co., 1942.

————. *Orlando*. New York: Harcourt, Brace and Co., 1928.

————. *A Writer's Diary*. New York: Harcourt, Brace and Co., 1953. Of great aid in understanding the friendship between these two writers. *Orlando* is especially illuminating for a "portrait" of V. Sackville-West.

Index

N.B. An asterisk in front of a name indicates a major fictional character in a novel or short story. I have not listed minor characters.